FIFTY PLACES TO

SKI &

SNOWBOARD

BEFORE YOU DIE

Downhill Experts Share the World's Greatest Destinations

Chris Santella

FOREWORD BY MATT HANSEN

ABRAMS IMAGE

NEW YORK

This book is for my girls, Cassidy, Annabel, and Deidre.

The Hatch Is On!

Why I Fly Fish:
Passionate Anglers on the Pastime's Appeal and How It Has Shaped Their Lives

Fifty Places to Bike Before You Die:
Biking Experts Share the World's Greatest Destinations

Fifty Places to Fly Fish Before You Die:
Fly-Fishing Experts Share the World's Greatest Destinations

Fifty More Places to Fly Fish Before You Die:
Fly-Fishing Experts Share More of the World's Greatest Destinations

Fifty Places to Play Golf Before You Die:
Golf Experts Share the World's Greatest Destinations

Fifty Favorite Fly-Fishing Tales:
Expert Fly Anglers Share Stories from the Sea and Stream

Fifty Places to Sail Before You Die:
Sailing Experts Share the World's Greatest Destinations

Fifty Places to Go Birding Before You Die:
Birding Experts Share the World's Greatest Destinations

Fifty Places to Dive Before You Die:
Diving Experts Share the World's Greatest Destinations

Fifty Places to Hike Before You Die:
Outdoor Experts Share the World's Greatest Destinations

Fifty More Places to Play Golf Before You Die:
Golf Experts Share the World's Greatest Destinations

Once in a Lifetime Trips:
The World's Fifty Most Extraordinary and Memorable Travel Experiences

Contents

Acknowledgments 8 / Foreword 9 / Introduction 11

THE DESTINATIONS

ACKNOWLEDGMENTS

This book would not have been possible without the generous assistance of the expert skiers and snowboarders who shared their time and experience to help bring these fifty great alpine venues to life. To these men and women, I offer the most heartfelt thanks. I especially want to thank Matt Hansen, a fine tarpon angler and ski writer who helped me polish off my figurative skies after a few years off the boards and made many fine introductions on my behalf. I also wish to acknowledge the fine efforts of my agent, Stephanie Kip Rostan; my editors, Jennifer Levesque, Samantha Weiner, and David Blatty; designer Anna Christian; and copyeditor Rob Sternitsky, who helped bring the book into being. Finally, I want to extend a special thanks to my wife, Deidre, and my daughters, Cassidy and Annabel, who've humored my absence during seemingly endless deadlines . . . and to my parents, Tina and Andy Santella, who are not skiers, but always encouraged me to pursue my passions.

FOREWORD

Growing up at the foot of the Wasatch Mountains in Utah, I was fortunate enough to have parents that encouraged skiing as a family activity. My brother, sister, and I often rode the bus to the world-class ski areas just a short distance away, an activity that fostered independence, adventure, and a thirst for powder. Those mountains rarely disappointed us, and even as youngsters, we knew we had it good.

It wasn't long before skiing turned into an obsession: the freedom and joy of speeding downhill over a snowy landscape, the raw beauty and challenge of being immersed in an unforgiving environment, and the bonds formed with friends and family during such life-changing experiences. Today, skiing defines much of my life. It's what I do with my family during the holidays, where I go on vacation, and how I make a living. But I never knew how deep it could take me until I stepped out of my comfort zone and started exploring new places.

During those early days of my youth, I believed all I needed was the Wasatch and later on, the Tetons. It's true that you could spend a lifetime in those snow-bound mountains and be perfectly content as a skier. But that ignores the size and breadth of our world. I've since learned that few things compare to the reward and exhilaration of sliding over snow as a traveler—experiencing the same liberating sensations of skiing but doing so in an altogether different place. Consider how much fun it is to ski at Alta, Utah, or Mount Baker, Washington, or Squaw Valley, California, and then do the same thing at, say, Zermatt, Switzerland. As skiers and snowboarders, we possess the tools to enter a community or mountain environment that can instantly feel like home, even if it is very far away and has its own distinct character.

I've also learned that no matter where you go—from the deep snows of Japan to the steeps of Chamonix or from the gritty ski bum culture of Silverton to the international flair of Portillo—skiers and snowboarders share the same language. They might use different words, and it might be untranslatable to English, but when their faces are plastered with fresh powder, or a big smile extends over their red cheeks at a bar, you understand them perfectly. And they understand you.

Ranking such locations is often an exercise in futility. Every ski area has its own merits—it often comes down to good snow and good people—but there are specific zones that hold great influence over the sport. In *Fifty Places to Ski and Snowboard Before You Die*, Chris Santella expertly compiles those areas into a comprehensive guide for skiers and snowboarders looking to make their own personal pilgrimage. From the little areas at the end of a country road to huge resorts full of nightlife and high-speed lifts, Santella makes it easy to dream of what adventures may wait. Each place has its own heartbeat, soul, and culture, and each helps define what it means to be a skier or snowboarder. Having experienced even a handful of them makes me forever grateful that my parents put me on skis all those years ago. By doing so, they introduced me to a world far bigger and more beautiful than I ever could have imagined.

So before your next adventure, go through this book and pick one . . . or pick them all. Either way, you'll know you've got it good.

—Matt Hansen

INTRODUCTION

For some, the coming of winter snow means the beginning of three (or four or six) months of self-imposed exile to the great indoors. For others, it's the time when the calendar really snaps to life.

I wrote *Fifty Places to Ski and Snowboard Before You Die* for those who appreciate the exhilaration of racing down a mountainside and the special sense of solitude that only an alpine snowscape can provide.

"What makes a destination a place you have to ski or snowboard before you die?" you might ask. "The chance to take in sweeping mountain scenery? To push your skills to the limit on dizzying steeps or monstrous moguls? To walk in the turns of some of the sports' most celebrated practitioners?" The answer would be yes to all of the above, and an abundance of other criteria. One thing I knew when I began this project: I was *not* the person to assemble this list. So I followed a recipe that served me well in my first nine *Fifty Places* books—to seek the advice of some professionals. To write *Fifty Places to Ski and Snowboard Before You Die*, I interviewed a host of people closely connected with the alpine world and asked them to share some of their favorite experiences. These experts range from celebrated Olympiads (like Jonny Moseley, Tommy Moe, and Billy Kidd) to equipment manufacturers (like Tait Wardlaw) to journalists (like Leslie Anthony). Some spoke of venues that are near and dear to their hearts, places where they've built their professional reputations; others spoke of places they've only visited once, but that made a profound impression. People appreciate skiing and riding for many different reasons, and this range of attractions is evidenced here. (To give a sense of the breadth of the interviewees' backgrounds, a bio of each individual is included after each essay.)

"Skiing" and "boarding" mean different things to different people. For some, it may mean a few runs on groomed cruisers before a leisurely lunch at an Austrian ski hut; for others, it may mean tracking fresh powder in the B.C. wilderness or taming seemingly impossible double black diamonds at Silverton. *Fifty Places to Ski and Snowboard Before You Die* attempts to capture the spectrum of alpine experiences. While the book collects fifty great ski/snowboard experiences, it by no means attempts to rank the places discussed, or the quality of the experiences afforded there. Such ranking is, of course, largely subjective.

In the hope that a few readers might embark on their own adventures, I have provided brief "If You Go" information at the end of each chapter, including the level of difficulty of each experience (based on information provided by ski areas/outfitters). The "If You Go" information is by no means a comprehensive list, but should give would-be travelers a starting point for planning their trip. (As lodging tastes/budgets may differ dramatically from individual to individual, I've tried to offer a general resource for lodging options. For some remote venues, there may be only one option, and it's been provided.)

Skiing and snowboarding can be risky pastimes, especially given some of the terrain extremely advanced practitioners will attempt to tackle. It should go without saying that skiers/riders should always use good judgment and know their limitations and wear a helmet . . . and that when skiing/riding in the backcountry, they should go with someone who knows the terrain, and carry necessary avalanche response equipment.

One needn't travel to the ends of the earth to find a rewarding alpine experience. A good dump of snow on your modest local hill can make for a great day. Yet a trip to a dream venue can create memories for a lifetime. It's my hope that this little book will inspire you to embark on some new skiing and snowboarding adventures of your own.

OPPOSITE:
Freestyle hero
Glen Plake makes
his way to the top
of Glacier Ronde
in Chamonix.
NEXT PAGE:
From the upper
reaches of Squaw
Valley, you can
spy brilliantly
blue Lake Tahoe.

The Destinations

CHUGACH MOUNTAINS

RECOMMENDED BY **Tag Kleiner**

Many off-piste enthusiasts dream of one day skiing Alaska—specifically the Chugach Mountains. Tag Kleiner was no different.

"I grew up watching ski films that profiled Alaska," he said. "The big, fast lines made an impression. It seemed like the promised land. I'd always wanted to go, but have to admit that I was scared. Over the time I've spent in the ski industry, I got to know Theo Meiners, who, along with Doug Coombs, pioneered heli-skiing in Alaska. I'd turned down invitations to ski the Chugach before, but when Theo invited me to come up, I decided to go. At the top of each run, I found my bottom cheeks puckering a bit with fear; at the bottom, I was ready to do it again."

The Chugach Range rests near the top of southeast Alaska and extends roughly three hundred miles, running west to east. Because of its proximity to the Pacific, the Chugach gets from thirty to eighty feet of snow a year—more snowfall than anywhere else in the world. Thanks to cold air that pours in from the Copper River Delta, the quality of the snow is exceptional. "There are several factors that make the Chugach—and more specifically, Alaska Rendezvous—a dream destination," Tag continued. "First, it's the Alaska terrain: big, long, steep ramps, steep couloirs and chutes, big open bowls, with lots and lots of snow. The amount of terrain is so vast, you lose all perspective. Think of it this way: Sun Valley, from top down, is 3,400 vertical feet. Some of the runs in the Chugach have five thousand vertical feet, almost twice as much . . . and they begin at a fifty-five- or sixty-degree pitch. It's frightening. Second, the lodge has an amazing group of guides. These folks live for this stuff. The love they have for Alaska skiing is contagious. They work hard to make you feel safe and keep you out of harm's way. Finally, the lodge is very close to the best skiing, and where it's situated [about forty-five miles up Thompson Pass from Valdez]

OPPOSITE:
A skier hits
a kicker on
a clear day in
the Northern
Chugach.

the weather is better than in Valdez. As a result, few ski days are lost because the helicopters can't fly. You're self-contained, with accommodations, restaurant, and bar. Many days, you can see the wall of clouds and fog that comes off the ocean and sits on Valdez. If you're flying out of there, you're sitting in your hotel. Where we are, it's blue skies. On my last visit, I had six potential ski days, and we flew all six days."

A few more statistics tell the rest of the story: Visitors to Alaska Rendezvous have access to more than 3,500 square miles of terrain; over the years, guests have skied more than 260 of the Chugach's almost infinite peaks. The terrain has the largest vertical relief of any accessible helicopter terrain in Alaska (while many mountains are not much taller than six thousand feet, much of each mountain is skiable vertically). Lastly, skiers will cover between twenty thousand and thirty thousand vertical feet on an average day!

Tag described the experience of off-piste skiing, Chugach-style. "The helicopter rides aren't very long because you're already so close to the mountains. Some of the ridges you land on don't seem big enough to support a helicopter. Once you get out of the copter and look at what it is you're going to ski, you want off. You're alone on the peak with your group and have to figure out how to get your gear on. Then the wait begins. Your guide goes first. You see him for about ten feet and then he's gone, disappearing because of the pitch of the slope and reappearing in the run-out five thousand feet later. When he reaches bottom, he'll radio up for the next person to come down. Your first turns are generally very steep—I remember a run called Happiness being especially steep. As soon as you make that first turn, you start working with the mountain. It gets very relaxing. You're making left turns, right turns, with a big smile on your face. As you get into it, your only concern is whether or not your legs will hold out. I learned a lot on my first trip to the Chugach. One of the best lessons I came away with is that you ski in the mountain, not *on* the mountain. You're in so much snow, and the pitch is so steep, it's better to think of it this way. If you keep your wits about you and make strong turns, it can be the most incredible skiing experience you'll ever have."

A few of the other runs you may have a chance to experience while visiting Alaska Rendezvous include Billy Mitchell (which rises in front of the lodge), Clue Land, and Candy Land. "When you ski Clue Land, you can see the Copper River way down in the valley below," Tag added. "You ski all the way down."

Tag Kleiner has many fond memories of skiing the Chugach. One involves a little inspirational chat. "I'll never forget one run I took with Theo Meiners as my guide. It was a little later in the week, and we'd been skiing progressively steeper and steeper terrain. We landed on a ridge, and after getting our gear on, Theo launched into what he must have considered to be a pep talk. 'What percent of Alaska ski terrain is avalanche terrain?' he asked. He answered his own question, 'A hundred percent. Everything you see is avalanche terrain. If it happens, it's a thirty-second event. You have to fight with all your heart for those thirty seconds if you're to have any chance to survive.' Then Theo turns around and is off down the mountain. I'm taking his talk in, looking at the other skiers, and thinking there's no way I'm going first. Then the radio crackles, and Theo calls up.

" 'Send Tag.' And I went."

Tag Kleiner is the global director of marketing at Smith Optics. Originally from Colorado, his skiing adventures have taken him all over the world to experience not only great skiing, but the amazing people that make the mountain lifestyle their passion. Tag currently lives in Ketchum, Idaho, with his nine-year-old son, Holden, and six-year-old daughter, Hazel, both of whom have been bitten by the ski bug.

If You Go

▶ **Getting There:** Greater Valdez is home base for skiing the Chugach Range; it's served by Alaska Airlines (800-252-7522; www.alaskaair.com). You can also fly into Anchorage and take a commuter flight with Era Alaska (www.flyera.com).

▶ **Season:** Alaska Rendezvous Lodge operates from the first week of March through the first week of May.

▶ **Lift Tickets:** A week at Alaska Rendezvous (888-634-0721; www.arlinc.com) begins at $6,500 and includes lodging and twenty-five thousand to thirty thousand vertical feet of skiing a day; shorter packages are available.

▶ **Level of Difficulty:** High. The sixty-degree inclines will intimidate most seasoned skiers.

TORDRILLO MOUNTAINS

RECOMMENDED BY **Tom Bie**

Corn snow in a wilderness setting. Opportunities to view Alaska's totemic wildlife. A pristine river teeming with trophy rainbow trout and king salmon. As the founder of a leading fly-fishing magazine and a former editor of a leading ski magazine, it's no surprise that Tordrillo Mountain Lodge's unique combination has some appeal for Tom Bie.

"Terrain-wise, with the glaciers and the access and the couloirs, nothing I've skied compares to Tordrillo," Tom declared. "You can find some really extreme terrain, as you'd expect. But many of the landing spots with challenging conditions have big bowls below that are ideal for less experienced skiers. Tordrillo is a place where skiers or snowboarders of modest ability can experience the thrill of heli-skiing."

And you might also get to meet and even ski with Tommy Moe, one of Tordrillo's owners, and an Olympic gold medal winner (Men's Downhill, Lillehammer, Norway, 1994).

Mention Alaska heli-skiing and it's the Chugach Range southeast of Anchorage (see page 17) that generally springs to mind. Tordrillo Mountain Lodge may change that. The Tordrillos are a compact range seventy-five miles northwest of Alaska's largest city. They rest between the Aleutian Range (to the south) and the Alaska Range (to the west and north), and span some sixty miles. Several peaks eclipse the eleven-thousand-foot mark. A combination of volcanic and glacial activity through the ages has carved an endless array of couloirs and towers; many runs range from three thousand to four thousand vertical feet. (One chute, which the guides have dubbed "Manhattan," is only fifty feet wide, and boasts one-thousand-foot walls.) With a yearly average of six hundred inches of fluffy snow and some 1.2 million acres of terrain to choose from, fresh powder (or in the spring, soft corn) is always in reach. On clear days—and there are a number of them—you can look out to see Denali (Mount McKinley) in the distance.

OPPOSITE:
The steeps
may make you
think twice, but
the corn snow in
spring is accom-
modating . . . and
many runs are but
a short flight away
from Tordrillo
Mountain Lodge.

21

Your home, as you explore the Tordrillo, is a five-thousand-square-foot log cabin set on the banks of Judd Lake and the Talachulitna River (which we'll return to later). You can look out at two eleven-thousand-foot volcanoes from the deck or from the lakeside wood-fired hot tub. During the latter part of the season, it's not uncommon to see black bears, moose, and occasionally even grizzlies foraging around the lake or exploring surrounding hillsides.

Tom described how a typical day of late-spring skiing unfolds in the Tordrillos. "In June, it's a pretty casual morning at the lodge. You want to give the snow some time to soften up, and the lodge is remote enough that you don't have to compete for runs. Generally, you're not in the helicopter until nine or nine-thirty. At Tordrillo Mountain Lodge, they use an AStar [that is, the Eurocopter AS350 B3e, known for its power, speed, and agility]. A ride in the AStar sets the tone for the day; it's safe to say that some people are more frightened by the ride than the skiing. AStars have a lot of glass. Pilots who've made it this far are extremely talented, and they like to show off a little. A guest sitting next to me—a guy who's done some skiing—grabbed my leg three times a day as we flew. I can't blame him—it's a little disconcerting as you fly along and suddenly a three-thousand- or four-thousand-foot cliff falls away.

"The first day out, you'll do a few warm-up runs so the guides can get a sense of how well you ski. On my last visit, I skied with Tommy Moe for several days. He's a hero to many people who followed his Olympic performance in 1994, and they'll invest a considerable amount of money just to be around him. For being such an accomplished skier, he's very patient, and has the perfect demeanor for talking to people. He and the other two owner-guides (Mike Overcast and Greg Harms) put everyone at ease; you'd follow them off a cliff if they told you to. Tommy has a way of assessing a group's skiing ability in a levelheaded manner. He wants to push people to help them improve their abilities, and he can throw out tips on technique without being at all condescending. It was funny—at one point, Tommy jumped a little ledge and went fifteen or twenty feet in the air. One of the visitors looked at me and said, 'How does he do that?' I replied that this is what downhillers do when they *retire*."

Despite the late start, spring skiers can expect to ski ten or twelve runs a day, with each run covering 1,500 to 3,000 feet. "You're in Alaska in June," Tom added. "You could ski all day and night. On my first day, it was 5:30 P.M. and we were still going. With the corn snow, even forty- to forty-five-degree drops did not seem too daunting."

Toward the end of the season, Tordrillo segues to a program that mixes spring skiing and fly-fishing—Cast and Carve. After a morning on the slopes, guests return to the lodge and swap skis/boards for fly rods and waders and climb back into the helicopter to explore the Talachulitna. "The lodge has several hybrid kayak-rafts that are rolled up and placed in the cage of the helicopter," Tom explained. "Then you take off downriver, looking for good spots to fish. Sometimes you can even spot pods of king salmon from the air. When you touch down, you pump up the rafts and float downstream, stopping to fish along the way. The Talachulitna is a very pristine river, like the upper Madison River in Yellowstone. It has beautiful rainbow trout; they jump like crazy. The salmon generally run fifteen to twenty-five pounds, and they're fresh from the sea. Both Tommy Moe and Mike Overcast grew up fishing and are expert kayakers, so the Cast and Carve is a natural for them."

TOM BIE is the founder, publisher, and editor in chief of *The Drake*, a respected fly-fishing journal started in 1998. Tom served as editor of *Powder* magazine from 2004 to 2007, and still pens ski-oriented pieces in addition to his fishing writing. Tom's ski travels have taken him from Alaska to the fjords of Norway to Chile to Soviet Georgia. He calls Colorado home.

If You Go

▶ **Getting There:** Guests gather in Anchorage, Alaska, which is served by many carriers, including Alaska Airlines (800-252-7522; www.alaskaair.com). From here, it's a forty-five-minute floatplane ride to Tordrillo Lodge.

▶ **Season:** Early February through April for ski packages; mid-June through early July for ski/fish packages.

▶ **Lift Tickets:** Seven days of skiing/lodging/transportation list at $11,000; a five-day Cast and Carve visit is $8,000.

▶ **Level of Difficulty:** While there are plenty of steep couloirs for the experts, the Tordrillos also have terrain well suited for intermediate skiers/boarders.

BANFF/LAKE LOUISE

RECOMMENDED BY **Dan Markham**

Banff National Park, with its monolithic mountains, shining glaciers, and abundant wild-life, is as beautiful an alpine area as one could hope for. For skiers and snowboarders, it's an added bonus that the park—which generally has strict limitations on commercial enterprise within its 2,564-square-mile area—is home to not just one, but three ski areas: Mount Norquay, the Lake Louise Ski Area, and Sunshine Village.

Dan Markham still recalls the first time he set eyes on the mountains of Banff. "I grew up ski racing in eastern Canada," he began, "and at one point, I came west to compete in a race at Mount Norquay. I remember looking up at the immense peaks as we made our way into the park, wondering how it would ever be possible to ski on these moun-tains . . . though I hadn't realized that these were just mountains, not ski areas. When we reached Norquay, I saw the lifts but still thought the mountain was a monster. It made an impression. I made my way to Calgary to go to university and raced up in Banff, and became an alpine ski instructor. After working around Calgary for a number of years, I eventually made the move to Banff—after getting engaged in Lake Louise and married in Banff! The ski areas at Banff have been part of my life for thirty-eight years!"

Banff is Canada's oldest national park, and was established in 1885; it comprises much of the southern section of the province of Alberta's border with British Columbia. That the region's famed hotels (Chateau Lake Louise and Banff Springs—not to mention the ski areas—exist in the national park is thanks in large part to the Canadian Pacific Railway and the laws of supply and demand. The railroad created a supply of westbound train seats from the eastern population centers; it was hoped that some recreational centers would create a demand. The railway did not underestimate Banff's appeal, and the park soon gained international recognition for its hiking, golf, and sightseeing. Its reputation for

OPPOSITE:

A boarder shreds
at Lake Louise,
one of "the Big 3"
at Banff.

skiing would come a few decades later. Mount Norquay was the first ski area in the Canadian Rockies, with its first runs cut in 1926, and a rope tow built in 1941. The first permanent lift at Sunshine Village was installed in 1945. Plans for a ski resort at Lake Louise were launched in the early 1930s, though the first lift didn't open until 1954.

Each of the three areas—which are marketed and operate under the umbrella of "Ski the Big 3"—has its unique appeal: Mount Norquay is a more intimate venue that's popular with Banff residents, and boasts night skiing; Sunshine Village rests at the highest elevation, and thus guarantees the most snow—an average of more than thirty feet; Lake Louise serves up the Big 3's most challenging steeps. But the eight thousand acres that the areas occupy share the distinction of being situated on a UNESCO World Heritage site, and that may be their most compelling quality. "There are many places where you can ski steeps and find great powder," Dan continued. "Look a little harder and you can find places with great terrain without lift lines. The areas around Banff have those things, but you also have this incredible interaction with Mother Nature, both in terms of animal life and unspoiled alpine terrain. We like to joke that, in Banff, the people are fenced in and the animals roam free. Elk and deer are as common around town as dogs and cats—this in part because the ungulates feel protected here from the wolf packs at either end of the valley. Sometimes you'll see wolves along the road; you're fairly certain to see mountain goats approaching Mount Norquay. In the early and late season—that is, before and after hibernation—it's not unheard of to see black and grizzly bears from the slopes. If you've had snow at night, everyone is out trying to get first tracks. I can't tell you how many times I've tried to get the first tracks, only to find I'd been beaten—there'd be cougar, elk, or wolf tracks on the hill.

"I like the fact that the resorts are not crowded with condos. That can create a feeling of congestion. Though Banff is definitely a tourist town, winter is our off-season. It's just not crowded. If you're into backcountry skiing, your options are endless. You can go up a chairlift, go through a gate to the backcountry, and you have thousands of acres where there's no mechanized access. Or you can drive along the road between Banff and Lake Louise, see a line you like, pull over, and off you go."

Like so many seasoned skiers, Dan has found himself seeking new challenges. After about fifteen minutes on a snowboard, he set his sights on telemarking, and that's where he's focused his energies the last ten years. "We're still a minority on most hills, the Big 3 included," he said, "but there's some great teleterrain at all three areas. Whitehorn

Chutes at Lake Louise is a series of consistent couloirs that fan out to nice powder. They're almost hourglass shaped. You can always get fresh tracks in there, though you have to let the chutes settle a few days after a big snow. Over at Sunshine Village, I like Bye Bye Bowl. It's a long, constant fall line with a concave roll near the top of the mountain. You can drop left or right; either way, you come down to a bowl. It faces south, and there's tremendous sunshine on a clear day. At Norquay, it's not the runs that get me so much as the social experience, especially at night. It's only five minutes from home. It's fun to see friends, grab a pint, and take a few runs."

Given Banff's unspoiled beauty, one can anticipate some tremendous views from the Big 3. "The alpenglow when the sun first breaks is beyond belief," Dan said. "At Sunshine, you see it reflecting off of Mount Assiniboine. At Lake Louise, it's best from the summit or near the Poma lift. When I see that early alpenglow, my day is made. Whatever happens after doesn't matter."

DAN MARKHAM has been skiing at the three resorts at Banff for almost forty years. He is a certified instructor in alpine and telemark skiing, and sits on the Canadian Avalanche Centre's board of directors, acting currently as vice president. After stints with various ad agencies, the Alberta premier's office, and the Canadian Pacific Railway, Dan now serves as director of marketing and sales at Ski Banff–Lake Louise–Sunshine.

If You Go

▶ **Getting There:** Visitors generally fly into Calgary, which has worldwide service on many major carriers. Banff and the Big 3 are a ninety-minute drive away.

▶ **Season:** The Big 3 ski season runs from mid-November to late May.

▶ **Lift Tickets:** Tri-area day tickets run $89.95 CAD; multi-day tickets are available. Tickets include night skiing at Mount Norquay and use of the shuttle service between the three hills. See details at www.skibig3.com.

▶ **Level of Difficulty:** The Big 3 offer varied terrain over almost eight thousand acres. Difficulty is rated 22 percent beginner; 45 percent intermediate; 33 percent advanced.

▶ **Accommodations:** You'll find a host of lodging options and packages at www.skibig3.com.

ANTARCTIC PENINSULA

RECOMMENDED BY **Doug Stoup**

"Antarctica is like a rose," adventurer Doug Stoup ventured. "There are many thorns, but its inner beauty is just insane. You can have forty-knot winds and temperatures of forty degrees below zero. But then again, where else can you ski down an empty mountain right to the sea and be greeted by scores of whales, hundreds of seals, and thousands of penguins? Over twenty-seven expeditions [to date], I've really fallen in love with the continent."

Antarctica is not one of the world's most welcoming places. This is evidenced by the fact that there are no indigenous people on the continent, despite the fact that it encompasses more than 5.5 million square miles, roughly 1.5 times the size of the United States! (A contingent of five thousand scientists from the twenty-seven nations that are signatories of the Antarctic Treaty maintain a year-round presence on the continent; another twenty-five thousand or so tourists visit each season.) A great majority of the landmass—an estimated 98 percent—consists of ice and snow that has an average thickness of seven thousand feet; scientists believe that up to 70 percent of the world's freshwater is contained here. Put another way: If the ice stored in Antarctica were to melt, the world's oceans would rise two hundred feet. While precipitation can reach the equivalent of thirty-six inches of water on the Antarctic Peninsula, the continent's wettest region, only an inch of precipitation reaches the South Pole. During the winter months, when temperatures hover in the balmy range of −40°F to −90°F, seawater surrounding the continent freezes up to two hundred miles offshore, covering an area even larger than Antarctica's landmass. In the summer (December through March), the freeze recedes, and a brief window opens for sailing to the more northerly portions of Antarctica. The continent is quite mountainous, with peaks (like Vinson Massif) more

OPPOSITE:
The odds of
finding another
skier on the
Antarctic
Peninsula are
fairly low . . .
though you may
get a first descent.

than sixteen thousand feet high; the lure of scaling a never-before-climbed peak has attracted many adventurers.

Given its location and inhospitable terrain, it's not surprising that the Antarctic continent went undiscovered until fairly recent times. Captain James Cook, in his relentless search for the "southern continent," crossed the Antarctic Circle in 1773 and again in 1774, though ice prevented him from ever reaching the landmass itself. (He did, however, come upon New Zealand and Tahiti on this voyage.) Sealers and whalers worked the icy waters around Antarctica in the early 1800s, and subsequent national expeditions sponsored by Britain and Russia confirmed that the landmass was indeed a continent and not merely a collection of islands. Over the next one hundred years, many expeditions were led to Antarctica. One of the most scientifically productive was the *Belgica* expedition, conducted by the Royal Geographical Society of Brussels in 1897–9; certainly the most famous was Sir Ernest Shackleton's 1914 attempt to cross the Antarctic continent on foot. (Despite having their ship *Endurance* crushed by pack ice some eighty miles offshore, Shackleton and his crew emerged after a twenty-month ordeal—including an eight-hundred-mile crossing in an open boat—with no loss of life.)

Suffice it to say, a ski trip to Antarctica is not well suited for the occasional traveler or casual alpinist. First, there's the crossing of the Drake Passage—almost five hundred miles, from Cape Horn to the Shetland Islands, at the northern tip of the continent. Whether you're on a larger, expedition cruise ship or the seventy-five-foot *Australis*, there's a sense of exploration as you pass through the Roaring Forties, the Furious Fifties, and the Screaming Sixties—the unobstructed winds that howl through the passage, where waves can reach heights of sixty-five feet. As you push farther south, you'll pass through alleys of icebergs—cracking, rolling, with massive chunks calving off. Upon reaching the islands surrounding the peninsula, you'll begin to encounter Antarctica's wondrous wildlife en masse. "Sometimes we'll stop on Livingston Island to visit an elephant seal, a gentoo penguin, and a giant petrel colony," Doug continued. "It's one of the few elephant seal colonies on the peninsula. There are thousands of the animals. The males can grow to be sixteen feet in length and weigh eight thousand pounds. The females can get to be ten feet long and seventeen thousand pounds in weight. The pups were just being born and it was amazing to watch." The seals, birds, and cetacean life are all fueled by incomprehensible amounts of krill, a tiny shrimplike crustacean that thrives in Antarctica's chilly, nutrient-rich waters.

As for the penguins: One thing that the National Geographic specials don't tell you is just how strong a colony of penguins smells!

"On a given trip, the boat will pull up at many different points along the Antarctic coast—sometimes islands, sometimes the mainland," Doug continued. "Skiers will put on skins, snowboarders will strap on snowshoes. We'll hike up a mountainside two thousand or three thousand feet. Oftentimes, there are descents on all sides, frequently right down to the water. Sitting atop that mountain, you're not in a hurry to descend. There are all sorts of birds flying about, whales breaching in the sea, which is blue with icebergs. It's so clean and pristine. Some of the descents have forty or fifty degrees of incline. It's a very special experience. With twenty hours of daylight, we have plenty of time to explore."

Over your week (or two weeks, depending on your trip), you will do some exploring. Each trip has a rough itinerary, but conditions—say, unexpectedly thick sea ice—require a level of flexibility.

One stop might include Wiencke Island. Here, you may ski a steep couloir named Wintervention; it was featured in the Warren Miller film of the same name. Another option on Wiencke is Noble Peak and the Sex Troll face (it's a long story). There's always the chance of a first descent. "On a 2010 trip, we found a beautiful couloir on the east side of Rongé Island, elevation seventeen thousand feet. We named it 'Directissima' (as we could see the *Aurora Australis* [Australia's Antarctic supply ship] at the bottom of the run), and it offered great snow conditions on a forty-five-degree sustained pitch all the way to the water." At the end of the day, you can toast your achievements with a libation cooled by ten-thousand-year-old glacial ice.

In a place as remote and unforgiving as the Antarctic Peninsula, visitors may face small hardships. Beyond plummeting temperatures, there's a decent chance you'll spend a few days stormbound in anchorage. And the snow may not always be the best. But how often can you make first tracks as you hear minke whales spouting in the near distance?

"I love leading trips to Antarctica, taking people to remote places that haven't been skied before," Doug added. "It's exciting to push the limits of human endurance. Most of the people who've gone consider it the trip of a lifetime. But I have many repeat clients. It makes that kind of impression."

DOUG STOUP is an expedition leader, polar guide, cinematographer, filmmaker, aerial rigger, ski and snowboard mountaineer, climber, motivational speaker, environmentalist, and educator. For more than ten years, he has been guiding teams across the frozen Arctic Ocean and Antarctica, from numerous "Last Degree" treks to his most recent 660-mile epic journey to the South Pole. Doug has received media coverage from CNN, the BBC, *Time* magazine, *Sports Illustrated Adventure*, and *National Geographic Traveler*. He was also featured in Warren Miller's film *Storm*. He is a member of the International Polar Guides Association, and is the owner of Ice Axe Expeditions (www.iceaxe.tv).

If You Go

▶ **Getting There:** Many ships heading for the Antarctic Peninsula depart from Ushuaia. Service is available via Buenos Aires on Aerolíneas Argentinas (800-333-0276; www .aerolineas.com.ar) and LAN (866-435-9526; www.lan.com).

▶ **Season:** Expeditions are generally planned for the early part of the austral summer—November, December, and January.

▶ **Lift Tickets:** Several companies lead ski/snowboard-oriented trips to Antarctica, including Ice Axe Expeditions (530-582-1246; www.iceaxe.tv). A berth in a lower-deck twin for a thirteen-day/twelve-night cruise begins at $8,990 per person. Longer itineraries are available.

▶ **Level of Difficulty:** The backcountry terrain is best suited for more experienced skiers/ boarders, though it's within the ability level of advanced intermediates.

TIERRA DEL FUEGO

RECOMMENDED BY **Daniel Griffith**

"There is a certain thrill in visiting Tierra del Fuego and Ushuaia," Daniel Griffith began. "You're at the southern tip of the Earth, the southernmost city in the world . . . and the southernmost ski resort. As you fly in, you see the Beagle Channel [named for Charles Darwin's boat] to one side and the Andes to the other. It's the only place where the Andes go west to east instead of north to south. It's such a wild place. As you look north and west, many of the mountains in your view have never seen footprints, let alone ski tracks. Though Ushuaia is a small city, the remainder of the area is undeveloped. It's a great place for an alpinist who wants an adventure."

Tierra del Fuego ("Land of Fire") rests at the bottom of the South American continent. ("Land of Fire," incidentally, stems from the campfires of the indigenous Yamana that European explorers spied from the sea.) Technically, it's an island of Argentine soil, separated from the mainland by the Strait of Magellan to the north and from the continent's most southern landmasses (under Chile's purview) by the Beagle Channel. (The fact that Ushuaia is one of the primary points of departure for Antarctica gives you a sense of just how far south it is!) Here, jagged mountains rise abruptly from the sea to heights of six thousand or seven thousand feet, and relentless winds blow across a rugged tundra. It's at once one of the most awe-inspiring and inhospitable (at least for humans) landscapes in the world. Cool temperatures year-round make for good and plentiful snow, though the snow and the skiing are only the beginning. "There are lots of places where you can find good skiing," Dan continued. "Ushuaia and Tierra del Fuego have an extra element in the culture, the flora, the fauna. These elements are the reason to go."

Dan likes to begin his Tierra del Fuego tours with a few days at Cerro Castor, the world's southernmost ski area. "Cerro Castor is a smaller resort in terms of its piste

terrain, and it's a great place to get our legs under us. It's a fairly low elevation, and that makes it easier for folks coming in from the East or West Coast of the United States or the United Kingdom. It also gives people more oxygen for the skinning that's to come. After a few runs, we'll head out the back gates to do some touring. We've skinned four or five hours and haven't run into anyone. I've taken groups up behind the resort, roughly a twenty-minute boot hike off the upper lift. You're at about 3,500 feet when you come off the lift and you gain another 650 feet. As you pass over the first rise, there are unbelievable volcanic rocks, covered with ice and moss. You go through a little passage with rock walls on each side, and it opens up to one of the most remarkable views. In one direction, there's the high Andes. Look north, and you can take in the fjords that you must cross to get back into Chile. You can also pick out the edge of the Bay of Ushuaia. I like to imagine the bay draining into the Beagle Channel and on to Cape Horn. The valleys are blanketed with impenetrable forests. It's such wild, spectacular terrain."

As Dan mentioned above, a big part of the allure of a trip to Tierra del Fuego is a chance to get a taste of the Land of Fire beyond the slopes. His itinerary includes a boat ride on the Beagle Channel where seals, sea lions, a variety of waterfowl, and occasionally even penguins are seen. Remnants of the communities of Tierra del Fuego's original inhabitants, the Yamana people, can be observed on Isla Bridges and in Tierra del Fuego National Park. Dan's favorite extracurricular activity is an evening of dogsledding and snowshoeing in the shadow of the Andes. "There's a local man who raises sled dogs," he explained. "He has a hundred huskies and malamutes, and has competed in the Iditarod. He gives us a demonstration of how the dogs are fitted to the sleds, with ten dogs per team. Then we divide into two groups. Half of us will don snowshoes and trek through a forest of lenga trees to a tepee on the tundra; the other half will ride out on the dogsleds. The hosts light a bonfire and serve guests hot chocolate with cognac while they share stories detailing the region's history. The guests who dogsledded out will snowshoe back and vice versa. When we get back to our lodge, there's a dinner of lentil and lamb stew waiting, along with bottles of Malbec and Cabernet Sauvignon. It's one of the highlights of the trip."

Certainly, one of the *on-the-mountain* highlights of Tierra del Fuego is the chance to climb and soar down Martial Glacier, which rests just north of Ushuaia. "There's a small family-run area near the base of the glacier, and we start by taking their ski lift up to gain the first nine hundred vertical feet," Dan said. "Then we put the skins on and glide to the

OPPOSITE:
Looking south
from the Martial
Glacier, you can
take in the city
of Ushuaia, the
bay of Ushuaia,
and the Beagle
Channel in
the distance.

Martial Glacier basin. You're looking at about 2.5 hours to reach the top. We're not trying to see how many runs we can squeeze in. Instead, we're focused on safety—how to use your shovel, avalanche transceiver, and probe, and depending on conditions we might use crampons, ice axes, or ski crampons. You will get a real taste of ski mountaineering as we practice self-arresting with ice axes and proper climbing techniques with crampons. The weather is ever-changing. It's not uncommon to have winds approaching seventy-five miles per hour—you know you're in Patagonia when those winds come up! You have to respect the terrain and the weather. You may have plans to ski a particular chute or couloir, but if it starts snowing hard or the fog drops down, you turn around. This is not sidecountry; it's true backcountry.

"Once we make it to the top, we hollow out a space to store our gear so it doesn't get blown away. I warn everyone to avoid going right to the ridge; an eighty- to one-hundred-mile-per-hour gust can push you off the back. We'll have a little snack and some yerba mate tea, pack up the skins, and get locked into our skis or snowboards. If it's clear, we'll want to drink in the view out over the city, the Bay of Ushuaia, and the Beagle Channel. There are several routes down. The more severe are forty-five to fifty-two degrees in pitch; for less experienced skiers/riders, there are routes with a thirty-two- to thirty-seven-degree pitch. In this maritime climate, the snow is similar to what you find in Alaska. The snow sticks to everything, and the glacier itself fills in nicely. It's a run of 3,500 vertical feet in all. About a third of the way down, there are two chutes and an hourglass-shaped couloir; sometimes it will have chalky conditions, sometimes powder. When you come out at the bottom section, you have a moderately pitched bowl. It's maybe three hundred turns. Depending on the day, it can be nice powder or corn.

"There are not a lot of places where you can ski down a glacier while you're looking out toward Cape Horn. It's quite an experience."

DANIEL GRIFFITH has twelve years of professional ski-guiding experience in the Wasatch Range of northern Utah and ten years of guiding experience in the Andes of Chile and Argentina. He has his Level I and Level II Avalanche Safety training certificates from the American Avalanche Institute and his Level III Avalanche Safety Certification from Swiss Rock Guides. He has completed his American Mountain Guides Association Ski Guides and Ski Mountaineering Courses, is a current member of the AMGA, and has been an avalanche field observer with the Utah Avalanche Forecast Center for the past five years. Dan is the owner and founder of Endless Turns (www.endlessturns.com), a ski and adventure travel company that leads guests to the Wasatch of Utah, the Andes of South America, and the European Alps. "For me, it's not just about the skiing/snow-boarding experiences," Dan said. "It's about getting to know the local people and their customs and traditions, learning new languages, eating wonderful cuisine, drinking fine wines, and discovering the amazing history behind each country."

If You Go

▶ **Getting There:** Guests generally reach Ushuaia via Buenos Aires. Service is available from Aerolíneas Argentinas (800-333-0276; www.aerolineas.com.ar) and LAN (866-435-9526; www.lan.com).

▶ **Season:** Mid-June to mid-October

▶ **Lift Tickets:** Endless Turns (www.endlessturns.com) leads weeklong tours exploring the piste/backcountry possibilities of greater Ushuaia. The trip, which includes hotels, lift tickets, transfers, meals, and guiding, is $2,880 per person.

▶ **Level of Difficulty:** The backcountry terrain is best suited for more experienced skiers/boarders, though it's within the ability level of advanced intermediates.

▶ **Accommodations:** If you go it alone, you can learn more about accommodation options in Ushuaia at www.tierradelfuego.org.ar.

KITZBÜHEL

RECOMMENDED BY **Atle Skårdal**

Before becoming chief race director for the Ladies' Alpine World Cup, Atle Skårdal was a back-to-back World Cup champion in the Super-G. When asked what mountain he recalled the most from his racing days, Atle did not hesitate. "The best memories from my racing career come from Kitzbühel," he enthused. "It's special in many different ways—its legacy, its place in the history of ski racing, the quality of the resort itself. And, naturally, the courses themselves. I first competed there in 1986, and then almost every year thereafter until I retired from racing in 1997. There was a special feeling I had each time I came to Kitzbühel, a combination of fear and excitement—really an unbeatable combination. I would start to feel it in my stomach when I saw the sign along the highway, and it would intensify when the mountain came into view, and I knew a big week was coming up."

Kitzbühel sits near the center of the Kitzbühel Alps in the western Austria province of Tyrol. Relative to some areas in the Alps, the peaks are of modest size, with Kitzbüheler Horn, the highest mountain, topping off at less than 6,600 feet. (Kitzbühel's lower elevation means that snow coverage can be a little iffy, especially on the lower sections of the area. Climate change may not bode well for future skiing.) Nonetheless, the area has come to play a central role in the world of international ski racing. It all started in 1892, when a local man named Franz Reisch came upon a book by polar explorer Fridtjof Nansen, titled *Across Greenland on Snowshoes*. The book mentioned Nansen's love of skiing, and Reisch, inspired by the notion, ordered a pair of wooden skis. Many of his contemporaries were dismissive of his efforts at this very new sport, but doubters were put in their place when Reisch made his way down from the summit of Kitzbüheler Horn. (According to the Kitzbühel Tourism Department, Reisch, in his enthusiasm, is said to have told a friend, "It was so beautiful that I have to slap you in the face!") Reisch wrote of his downhill experience in the first edition of *Der Schneeschuh* (The Snowshoe) magazine, and the seeds for Kitzbühel's skiing future were planted. By 1895, regular ski races were being held, and by 1902, the Kitzbühel Winter Sports Association was founded; it was rechristened the Kitzbüheler Ski Club in 1931.

It was also in 1931 that the first race was held on Hahnenkamm (Rooster's Comb), perhaps the most famed hill at Kitzbühel. Over time, the race has expanded into a series of races known as the Hahnenkammrennen, now a fixture on the men's alpine World Cup circuit. Tens of thousands of fans gather on the slopes each January to take in the Super-G, Slalom, and Downhill; 250 million other enthusiasts follow the event on television.

The Hahnenkammrennen's downhill course—the Streif, or "streak"—is one of the most famous racing trails in the world . . . and among the most demanding. (It's been used for the downhill since the early days; its name stems from the Streifalm pastures, which were once located in the upper part of the course.) The data points give pause: jumps up to 260 feet, steeps to 85 percent, and speeds to 87 miles per hour, with an average speed of 64 miles per hour. The Streif's diversity makes it a classic, and it seems each stretch has a name. As described in the Kitzbühel ski program, it includes "steep edges that result in high jumps at high speeds, steep downhill portions, tricky straight downhill racing sections, curves and bends, gliding tracks, undulating terrain, and even a short uphill passage right before the Seidlalm jump . . . the most difficult parts of the run are the straight section at the beginning, the Mausefalle jump, the steep Steilhang slope, the Hausberg edge, the traverse, and the final straight section." Except during the weeks before the Hahnenkammrennen, the Streif is open for advanced skiers (it's recommended that you sharpen your edges before taking it on). Even skiers of more modest abilities can have a moment in the limelight on the "Family Streif," which bypasses the course's most challenging elements.

"As you come out of the starter's hut, you're shocked at how steep it is at the outset," Atle described. "In competition, you're supposed to push as hard as you can out of the gate, though your instinct makes you want to go slow. Once you leave the starting gate, you begin to feel relieved and start to have fun. Pretty soon you're straight into business. There's no time to reconsider, you just go with the flow."

Kitzbühel is the center of the competitive racing world for the last few weeks of January, though for the remainder of the winter season, it attracts skiers and boarders whose main objective is less about victory and more about fun. Despite the notoriety of Streif and Ganslernhang (the Hahnenkammrennen's famed slalom course), much of the area—more than eighty miles of trails—is given over to beginner and intermediate terrain. For many visitors, a stay at Kitzbühel is about going slow, rather than going fast. There are fifty-six ski "huts" scattered among the area's six sections (Hahnenkamm, Bichlalm, Resterhöhe, Pengelstein, Gaisberg, and Kitzbüheler Horn), and a leisurely lunch in one of these comfortable lodges is almost a given. "If there's one dish that you'll never forget in Austria, it's the Wiener schnitzel," Atle said. "They're famous for it." (The breaded and fried veal is indeed the Austrian national dish.) A few favorites on Hahnenkamm include Berghaus, Tyrol, and Hahnenkammstüberl; on Resterhöhe, Hanglalm and Bruggeralm come well recommended; on Pengelstien, Usterweis gets good ratings; and on the Horn, Hornköpfl-Hütte receives praise. When you come off the slopes, Kitzbühel is not the sleepy town its medieval architecture might hint at. There's a bustling nightlife that includes several discos.

"Austria sets very high standards for its hotels and food," Atle added. "The complete package is hard to beat for a good ski vacation."

ATLE SKÅRDAL has been involved with alpine skiing since he was four years old. During his racing career, Atle won the overall World Cup title in Super-G, became a back-to-back Super-G World Champion in the years 1996 and 1997, and won the silver medal at the downhill race during the World Championships in 1993, among other victories. He ended his career after the 1996-97 season, and became head coach for the Norwegian National Ski Team. Since 2005, he has worked with FIS as chief race director for the Ladies' Alpine World Cup. While the director position is a year-round job, the summer season is slightly more relaxed. In between his slope inspection trips and the preparation for the upcoming season, Atle spends what he calls his "protected time" fishing and eating plenty of seafood on the coastline of his home country, Norway. "When I get the chance to go skiing, my mind still believes I am able to race down the slope as well as I used to, but my legs seem to disagree," Atle shared.

If You Go

► **Getting There:** Kitzbühel is roughly sixty miles from Innsbruck, which is served by Austrian Airlines (+43 5 1766 1000; www.austrian.com) and British Airways (800-247-9297; www.ba.com).

► **Season:** Kitzbühel usually opens by early November and closes in late April.

► **Lift Tickets:** Adult day tickets are 41.50 euros. Multi-day tickets are available.

► **Level of Difficulty:** Kitzbühel (www.kitzbuehel.com) has terrain for everyone. The area's 125 miles of terrain are rated as follows: 33 percent beginner; 39 percent intermediate; and 28 percent expert.

► **Accommodations:** Kitzbühel Tourism (+43 5356 66660; www.kitzbuehel.com) lists the many lodging options available in Kitzbühel and the neighboring towns of Reith, Aurach, and Jochberg.

DESTINATION 6

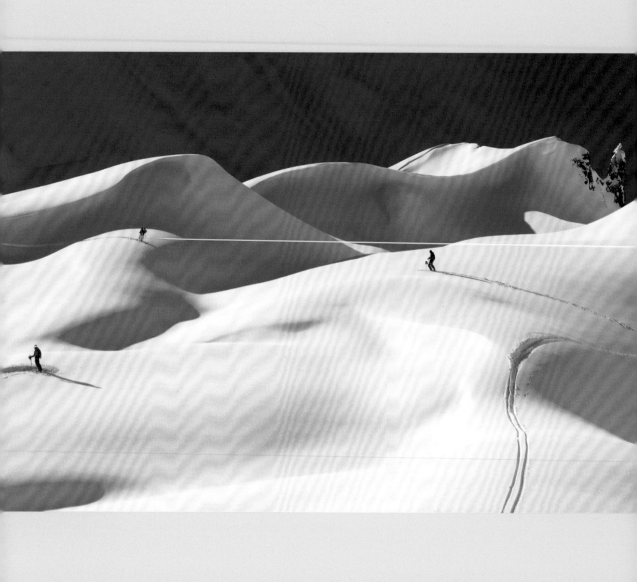

ST. ANTON

RECOMMENDED BY **Geli** AND **Stefan Häusl**

Some venture to St. Anton to ski in the footprints of some of the sport's earliest pioneers. Others come to partake of the resort's famed off-piste powder . . . or to revel in the village's infamous après-ski scene.

Few go home disappointed!

"The mountains around St. Anton were simply made for skiing," Stefan Häusl said. "We're famous for our tree skiing and off-piste terrain in general, but the mountains also offer all sorts of piste terrain. It's like a big playground. You can go up one slope and ski down into a whole different valley—sometimes you'll have to take a taxi back to town. If you go down the wrong side of the mountain in New Zealand, it might take you a year to get back."

"At St. Anton, you don't have one big bowl facing in one direction," Geli Häusl chimed in. "You can always find good snow if you shift to terrain that has a different exposure. What makes St. Anton special is that the love of skiing that brings people here is a great equalizer. We have a reputation for attracting royalty and jet-setters. But once you have your helmet and goggles on, everyone is the same, from the royals down to the ski bums. They're all here to enjoy the same terrain."

St. Anton, like Kitzbühel (page 38), is situated in the Tyrol province of western Austria. It is both a town and a ski mountain, as well as the catchall name for a collection of areas in the Arlberg mountain range that include St. Anton, St. Christoph, Stuben, Zürs, Lech, Oberlech, and Sonnenkopf. St. Anton am Arlberg is nothing if not vast—the combined area includes 160 miles of groomed trails, 114 miles of off-piste terrain, 82 lifts, and nearly 5,000 feet of vertical drop from Valluga, the region's highest peak at 9,222 feet. (Skiers and boarders can explore all the Arlberg region's slopes under one pass.) St.

OPPOSITE:
Lots of different
exposures mean
a constant supply
of good snow at
St. Anton . . .
if you can pull
yourself out of
MooserWirt.

7
DESTINATION

Anton am Arlberg has a rich ski pedigree; the region's first ski club was formed in 1901, and its first races were held in 1903. One of the events was won by a twelve-year-old boy named Hannes Schneider. A few years later, at the age of sixteen, Schneider became a full-time ski instructor at the Hotel Post in St. Anton and began developing the instructional technique that would come to be known as the Arlberg method. The technique—which takes new skiers from a simple snowplow to a stem christie turn and onto a parallel turn—was developed to give new skiers more control on the slopes. Schneider opened the Ski School Arlberg in 1921. That same year, he starred in what would become the world's first instructional ski film. The film—and a subsequent book, *The Wonders of Skiing*—helped establish the Arlberg method around the world. His techniques are still in wide use today.

Stefan described how he might show off St. Anton's alpine amenities to a visitor. "I'd pick up my guest at their hotel and walk to one of the lifts. The village has a large pedestrian zone, and the lifts are all in walking distance. I'd probably go up the Galzig lift, as the sun is on the slopes here in the morning. Assuming that my companion is an average piste skier, we might head up to Valluga, the highest point reachable by lift. There are beautiful views out over the valley from there. We'd take a red (intermediate) slope down; it's a 4,500-foot vertical drop if you go all the way down to the village, so you need to have some thighs! Next, we'd take the Kapall lift. The 2001 world championships were held here, and you can ski the men's/women's downhill run. Next, we'd break for lunch. There are many options on the mountain and in the village. One I like is Café Anton, right at the bottom of the Galzig lift. They have good food and coffee and the people are very friendly. After lunch, we'd head to the Rendl lift, as this part of the area faces the west. We'd take some runs here and maybe stop to watch the freeskiers and snowboarders on the jumps and rails in the fun [terrain] park there. If it's later in the season or a sunny day, we'd definitely visit Rendl Beach. There are deck chairs set out there for people to enjoy the sun.

"More experienced skiers come to St. Anton to ski the off-piste terrain, and there's a great deal available. Perhaps the most famous of these is the run from the top of Valluga to Zürs; you're skiing the backside of the mountain. You need to be accompanied by a guide, take a gondola up the final section of Valluga, and then hike up to the very top. It's extremely steep. Quite a few people who go up to do the run look over the edge, get a bit of a tummy ache, and ride the gondola back down. People who can make the run are proud to tell their friends they went from Valluga to Zürs on skis." Other well-regarded off-piste trails include Bachseite, Zwischen, Schindlerhang, and Black Osthang.

One St. Anton must for anyone the least bit interestest in après-ski activity is an afternoon stop at the MooserWirt, perhaps the Alps' most famous—or infamous—slope-side watering hole. (It's situated at the bottom of Blue run number one, off the Zammermoos chair.) Here's how English ski blogger Sidney Reilly described the scene at MooserWirt:

> It sells more beer per square meter than anywhere else in Austria and it has the worst euro trash music on the mountain unless you are German. . . . The food is very good and the portions very large so it is a good bet for lunch but be warned in peak season it will be very busy. But from 3pm onwards the crowds really start to arrive and by 4pm you have no chance of finding a seat as the music booms out across the piste. To truly enjoy the Mooserwirt experience I would suggest that you get there early (ideally book a table) and watch what happens at 3:30 when they start the "Final Countdown," the electronic shutters all close, the amazing light show starts and the crowds pour in. . . . Very soon the place is packed, literally to bursting point with very loud, beer drinking skiers all singing along to the mostly naff [i.e., tacky] German dance music.

"I don't know exactly how it works," Geli offered, "but every day it does. When that song comes on, everyone gets up on their chairs, and it's crazy from the first song to the last."

STEFAN HÄUSL was born in Salzburg, Austria, and grew up in Saalfelden. He started skiing at the age of three and soon became a ski racer. At age eighteen, Stefan started his ski instructor and ski-guiding exams. When he completed his training, he started as an examiner for the top-level ski instructors in Austria. He moved to the Arlberg region and worked for the Ski Akademie St. Christoph. In 1999, he won the Powder 8 World Championships held in Canada. In 2000, he was third in that competition. As the free-riding scene in Europe started to grow, he began to compete in that realm, learning how to drop off cliffs and ski big lines. He has been a professional freeride skier since 2005. In 2011 he won the first Freeride World Tour stop in Austria. He lives near St. Anton with his wife, Geli, and their daughter, Jana. Learn more about Stefan at www.stefan hausl.com.

ANGELIKA "GELI" HÄUSL grew up in the Arlberg region of Austria. After a brief career as a hairdresser, she began her ski-instructing exams, and has been teaching/guiding since 2004. Geli had a successful career as a professional freerider, winning the 2003 New Zealand National Freeride Competition, the 2003 New Zealand Base Ultracross Series, and the 2007 Snowfever in Fieberbrunn, Austria. She finished third on the 2005 Freeskiing Euro Tour. Geli has skied around the world, including Nepal, Tibet, Alaska, Greenland, New Zealand, Argentina, and Iran. She's been featured in two movies, *Elements* and *Headscarf vs. Beanie* (about her travels in Iran). She now works as a guide in St. Anton and also operates a ski school. She lives near St. Anton with her husband, Stefan, and their daughter, Jana. Learn more about Geli at www.geliskiing.com.

If You Go

▶ **Getting There:** St. Anton is roughly sixty miles from Innsbruck, which is served by Austrian Airlines (+43 5 1766 1000; www.austrian.com) and British Airways (800-247-9297; www.ba.com).

▶ **Season:** St. Anton's season runs from November 30 to April 21.

▶ **Lift Tickets:** Adult lift tickets are 47 euros, and provide access to St. Anton, St. Christoph, Stuben, Zürs, Lech, Oberlech, Klösterle, and Sonnenkopf. Multi-day passes are available. See details at www.skiarlberg.at.

▶ **Level of Difficulty:** St. Anton offers terrain suited to a host of ability levels, and is classified as follows: 41 percent beginner; 48 percent advanced; 11 percent expert.

▶ **Accommodations:** St. Anton am Arlberg Tourism Office (+43 5446 22690; www.stantonamarlberg.com) lists the region's many lodging options.

BUGABOOS

RECOMMENDED BY **Fred Noble**

What follows is an example of the kind of devotion heli-skiing in the Bugaboos can inspire:

"I started skiing when I was sixteen," Fred Noble began, "and I always wanted to be in the backcountry. The feeling of isolation, untracked powder snow—it captivated me. After high school, I ski-bummed around the west, visiting ski meccas like Sun Valley, Alta, and Aspen. Subsequently, Squaw Valley, Vail, Jackson Hole, and Snowbird came onto the scene. I immediately headed out to these areas even before there was a book called *Fifty Places to Ski and Snowboard Before You Die*.

"I started working at a real job, and one day I saw an ad for heli-skiing at $55. That was a lot of coin considering I paid $2.50 for an all-day pass at Alta. Nevertheless, this could be a possibility if I brown-bagged my lunch every day and sold pop bottles. Eventually, I saved enough to head out for the epic ski adventure of a lifetime.

"I loaded my 1958 Volkswagen Beetle with skis, sleeping bag, some cheese, crackers, carrots, and celery, and left Oregon for Valemount in Canada. Fortunately, the VW got thirty-five miles per gallon at thirty cents a gallon. After driving for seventeen hours straight, I arrived at two A.M. and bedded down, barely sleeping, in anticipation of the adventure to come.

"Wide awake at six A.M., I wandered around until I found a door that said MANAGER. I knocked lightly several times without a response. Impatiently I knocked louder and more frequently until a sleepy-eyed, gruff individual asked, 'What do you want?' In my most enthusiastic and cheerful voice I said, 'I'm here to go heli-skiing!' He promptly told me to go away and shut the door. I headed back to the car for a breakfast of celery and carrot sticks. An hour later I saw activity in the building and approached the manager once

again, proclaiming, 'I'm here to go heli-skiing!' Perturbed by my unbridled enthusiasm, he dismissed me again while finishing his breakfast.

"Meanwhile, a few people had gathered in the parking lot. It began pouring down rain. The manager finally came out. 'We are not skiing today,' he said. 'It's raining.' 'You're kidding me,' I replied. 'I drove seventeen hours to get here.' He went back inside and the group of would-be skiers started to pack their cars. At this point, I was determined to not drive all the way back to Portland without skiing, so I asked everyone if they would be willing to ski if I could convince the manager to take us. All of them were from Seattle and were not strangers to wet snow and agreed to my plan. I went back to the manager and said I had nine eager skiers. 'The skiing is terrible, and you are crazy,' he said. 'We have the money,' I replied. Finally, he acquiesced with the caveat that if we didn't like it there would be no refunds.

"We flew out of Valemount over these incredibly pristine mountains. When we sat down, the snow was soggy but I didn't care; at least it was untracked. The guide was giving safety instructions but I was not listening because I was mesmerized by the vast expanse of untracked snow. Following the guide's instructions, the group started their descent. I spied a small cliff to the right, hiked over and hucked myself off. Much to my chagrin, the guide caught my antics and royally chewed me out for not following instructions. We made a couple more runs in the rain, whooping and hollering while the guide was wondering, *Who are these crazy people?*

"I came back a month later with a group of friends and met Hans Gmoser, who'd gotten wind of my rainy-day adventure. He asked how I knew all these people, and would I like to work for him. I told him I had a job and declined. A few weeks later I returned with another group. At the end of a season I received a small check from Hans. I called and asked what gives. He told me that the check is my commission for bringing people to Canadian Mountain Holidays. At first I told him to take it back and put it toward more skiing. He told me to keep the check and keep on doing what I was doing. I told Hans that if I was going to represent CMH, I needed to get into the lodges to meet the managers and see how the operation works. He told me that he couldn't guarantee skiing. I told him I didn't need to ski and that it was essential that I make the rounds. That apparently sealed the deal, no paperwork, no contract, just a handshake and a declaration that as long as I was having fun I would stay on. It's been thirty-eight years and I am still here."

OPPOSITE:
Endless fresh lines await in the shadow of the granite spires of the Bugaboos.

The Bugaboos—and Bugaboo Lodge—hold an iconic place in the world of backcountry and heli-skiing. After all, it was here that Hans Gmoser pioneered the notion of bypassing the folderol of a lift and using a whirlybird instead to take skiers (and much later, boarders) to places that no lift could ever go. An Austrian immigrant, Gmoser got his start guiding climbers and skiers in the wilderness surrounding Mount Assiniboine, just west of Banff National Park, under the auspices of Canadian Mountain Holidays. The heli-ski notion came to fruition in 1965; by 1968, his first mountain lodge in the Bugaboos had been established. Today, CMH operates eleven lodges in the mountains of eastern British Columbia.

It's no surprise that the Bugaboos, located in the Columbia Mountains of B.C. and the heart of the Purcells, got Hans Gmoser's attention. First, the Bugaboos are extremely isolated, promising plenty of solitude; over five hundred square miles and two-hundred-plus runs are available to explore. Second, like the other ranges in the area, they see a tremendous amount of snow, an average of more than four hundred inches a year. Finally, there's the terrain, highlighted by the majestic granite spires that define the area for anyone who's visited . . . or dreamed of visiting. Topher Donahue described it beautifully in his book, *Bugaboo Dreams*: "In the surrounding mountains, the glaciers shaped the softer sedimentary rocks as well, but left more rugged faces as if the carving force of the glacier were in the hands of a drunk with a bulldozer. The tectonic intrusion that pushed the granite into the sky also lifted the surrounding area into a high plateau, creating deep valleys on all sides and ski runs that begin within snowball-throwing distance of the surreal rock walls and go for miles down rolling steep glaciers into uninhabited valleys."

After almost fifty years, CMH has a well-established routine at Bugaboo Lodge. "The guides check the weather and snow conditions early in the morning, and determine what areas will be safest and provide the best snow," Fred continued. "There are down days, but they're extremely infrequent. Having so much experience in the area, the pilots and guides understand the microclimates here and can usually find someplace where conditions will be right. [If you don't get in the guaranteed amount of vertical footage—say, a hundred thousand vertical feet for a seven-day excursion—you'll receive a refund of $120 for each 3,280 feet (1,000 meters) you missed.] In the early winter, you'll generally get in four to six runs before lunch. The helicopter may have to refuel at this point. Groups—usually one guide and eleven skiers—will eat outside; if anyone is tired, they can return to the lodge. When I started doing trips, lunch was a bologna sandwich and an orange.

Now it includes hot soup, hot tea, an exotic sandwich, tins of sardines, smoked oysters, fruit, and a variety of homemade cookies prepared by our in-house baker. In the afternoon, you'll get in another four to six runs. In the spring, with longer days, fifteen to twenty runs a day is the norm."

Over the years, Fred has logged close to eight million vertical feet in the Bugaboos and other CMH properties. In 2010, at the age of seventy-three, he was diagnosed with ALS (Lou Gehrig's disease) and confined to a wheelchair. That has not taken "The Fredinator" off the slopes. On March 24, 2012, he made the first sit-ski descent in the Bugaboos.

FRED NOBLE has been skiing since the age of sixteen, and was Canadian Mountain Holidays' first North American representative. He's worked with the company for thirty-eight years. Fred's travels have taken him to eighty-five countries and countless ski mountains. Though "The Fredinator" has contracted ALS, he remains active, raising money to fund ALS research through bike rides (with an arm-powered bike) and a ski event at Mount Hood called Ski to Defeat ALS. Learn more about Fred's achievements at www.frednobleadventure.com.

If You Go

▶ **Getting There:** Guests fly into Calgary, Alberta, which is served by most major carriers. From here, a bus will take you to the helipad, where a waiting copter will spirit you to the lodge.

▶ **Season:** Canadian Mountain Holidays' Bugaboo Lodge operates from December 20 through May 4.

▶ **Lift Tickets:** Weeklong packages at Canadian Mountain Holidays' Bugaboo Lodge (403-762-7100; www.canadianmountainholidays.com) range from $6,935 to $11,525 (CAD). Skis tailored for the Bugaboos' snow are provided.

▶ **Level of Difficulty:** Visitors should ski/board at an intermediate level, at least, and preferably have deep-powder experience . . . though CMH's guides can help you get up to speed fairly quickly.

KOOTENAY

RECOMMENDED BY **John Laing**

Nelson, a town in the Kootenay region of southeastern British Columbia that's been shaped as much by its silver-rush past as its (reputed) cannabis-growing present, is a hub for snowcat- and heli-skiing operations in the surrounding Kootenay Range of the Selkirk Mountains. For John Laing, the Nelson cat-boarding experience is defined by Baldface Lodge. "The way Baldface has embraced the sport of snowboarding makes it special," he began. "You're a helicopter or a cat ride away from civilization, far-removed from the hype that's come to surround the sport. You're hanging with a small group in the middle of nowhere, embracing what snowboarding is all about. All the guests and guides during a given week grow to depend on each other—though the riding is not as steep as in some places, there's always potential for avalanches. When you're back in the lodge at the end of the day, looking at photos and film of the day's experiences, you feel like, *Yes, this is why we do this. The soul of the sport, the passion is there.*"

Baldface Lodge was the brainchild of Jeff Pensiero, a former snowboard rep, who set out to find a spot in interior B.C. to establish a cat-boarding lodge. He (along with his wife, Paula, and a college pal, Jim Fraps) found a spot across Kootenay Lake from Nelson—either a ten-minute helicopter ride if the skies are clear or a slightly longer boat ride and snowcat conveyance if the weather is in. The site, which sits at an elevation of 6,750 feet among the jagged peaks of the Kootenay, boasts five peaks linked by a ridge-line; the highest peak the Baldface cats reach is at 7,678 feet. With financial support that included two members of the rock band the Foo Fighters (whose investment helped buy Baldface's first cat) and the promotional support of snowboarding legend Craig Kelly (before his death in 2003), the lodge became a reality. Today, guests have access to more than thirty-two thousand acres of terrain through some one hundred miles of cat trails.

OPPOSITE: Baldface Lodge's squad of snowcats can definitely spirit you to fresh snow, though you should have some familiarity with deep powder skiing/riding before you arrive.

With an average of five hundred inches of snow a year, finding fresh powder poses little challenge, though finding the stamina to ride down through twenty thousand vertical feet of it a day may prove daunting to some.

"I have to tip my hat to Jeff and his team," John continued. "They really understand what the region's mountains have to offer for the backcountry snowboarder. Beyond the tremendous terrain and the very comfortable lodge, Jeff has assembled a great team of guides. In my experience, Canadian backcountry guides are the best. For them, safety is the first priority in guiding. In Canada, guides need to attend a two-week course on Kokanee Glacier just to reach Level I certification. The guides at Baldface can tell you at five A.M. what the snow will be doing at nine A.M." John went on to describe a typical day at Baldface.

"A buffet breakfast is placed out at seven A.M. Before or after, you have the option to do some yoga to loosen up; the lodge has an instructor on staff. You pack your own lunch, which you place in a bin with your other gear, which is then placed in the snowcat. Then you're off. On your first day, the guides will give you a refresher course on using a transceiver, including some hands-on training. There are never too many times that you can be refreshed about avalanche safety. The first run, you follow your guide closely as he checks out the snow. After that, it's game on."

Given the terrain and the demands of the Kootenay's extreme powder, Baldface boarding may not appeal to everyone. The lodge's website states that

> if you have never skied powder or shy away from it at your local resort, this is not the place to learn. If you are expecting to ski 50-degree shoots and huck 30-foot airs every run you will be disappointed. We only ski this type of terrain when conditions and group abilities allow. To increase your opportunity to ski and ride expert terrain, book an entire snowcat with like-minded friends and we'll do our best to take you on our most exciting (but safe) runs.

Even with these caveats, most agree that Baldface offers a special experience. "During my visits, we averaged about twelve runs a day," John said. "There are a few runs that have stuck in my mind. One is out to the north, an area called the Burn. It's a mountainside that went up in flames some years ago; you ride a long, steep path through a forest of ghostly trees. You can run your finger along a tree and still get soot on your glove. Another is Cheeky Monkey. It stands out for its steepness, top to bottom, though there are some nice pillows in the run." During the day, each cat is accompanied by a photographer, who captures some of the day's best moments. Once you've returned to the lodge, drinks, hot appetizers, and massages await. Before dinner is served, everyone gathers by the big screen for a slide show of the day's photos.

Well-appointed accommodations, nice amenities (including a sauna), and deep powder all make for a memorable visit. But for John Laing, what makes Baldface special is the people. "They have a big staff at Baldface, and everyone—from the guides to the kitchen staff—is passionate about snowboarding, and this enhances the experience. On one occasion, I happened to be there on Craig Kelly's birthday. He was considered a god of the Kootenays—still is, almost ten years after his death. Some of the younger snowboarders don't know much about the pioneers, what they did to help establish the sport. At Baldface, he is remembered with reverence."

JOHN LAING is a senior editor at *Frequency: The Snowboarder's Journal*. Snowboarding has taken him all over the world.

If You Go

▶ **Getting There:** Visitors from the United States generally fly to Spokane, Washington, and either rent a car for the 3.5-hour drive to Nelson, B.C., or take a shuttle offered by Classic Limousine (509-924-4194). Baldface will arrange transport from Nelson. Spokane is served by several carriers, including Alaska Airlines (800-252-7522; www.alaskaair.com) and Delta Airlines (800-221-1212; www.delta.com).

▶ **Season:** Baldface generally operates from mid-December to early April. Late January through mid-March usually offers the best snow.

▶ **Lift Tickets:** Packages that include five nights of lodging and four days of cat skiing range from $2,094.34 to $4,347.81 (CAD), depending on accommodation type and time of year. See details at www.baldface.net.

▶ **Level of Difficulty:** You'll cover at least fifteen thousand feet of vertical a day; Baldface recommends you have at least intermediate/advanced-level powder skills.

▶ **Accommodations:** Guests at Baldface Lodge can opt to stay in the main lodge or one of seven chalets.

DESTINATION 9

THE SELKIRKS

RECOMMENDED BY **Lyndell Keating**

"First, I have to say that I really love snowcat skiing," Lyndell Keating enthused. "It's very hard to find a resort where you can get amazing powder and fresh line after fresh line. If you're cat skiing, it's guaranteed. When you're cat skiing, you don't have to elbow your way off the chairlift to get to good snow. All the powder is there for the taking.

"To me, all cat skiing is fantastic. But after all of my travels over the years, Selkirk Wilderness Skiing is my favorite. There's something magical about this operation. The founder, Allan Drury, pioneered snowcat skiing in British Columbia back in 1975. They've had a lot of time to perfect things!" Selkirk Wilderness is doing something right: More than half of their guests have skied with them for more than ten years.

It was an oil-industry boondoggle that helped give birth to British Columbia's snowcat scene. In the winter of 1969/70, Drury was invited to take a spot on a promotional heli-ski week sponsored by Bow Helicopters when more-senior executives at his company balked at what seemed a preposterously edgy endeavor. This experience—and a similar trip the following year—got him thinking about the possibilities. Recalling how snowcats had been used to convey skiers to areas soon to be served by lifts at Aspen, Drury contacted Bombardier (a major manufacturer of cats for trail grooming at the time) and the company agreed to sell him a twelve-passenger cat with a major improvement over the cats at Aspen: an enclosed cab. With conveyance in place, Drury and his wife, Brenda, began seeking the right spot to establish their operation, and landed in the Selkirks, sixty miles north of Nelson, on Meadow Mountain. The original farmhouse has been replaced by a comfortable lodge (with hot tub, sauna, and massage facilities) that can accommodate twenty-four guests, but the panoramic views of the Purcells and Selkirks have remained the same . . . though sadly, Allan Drury passed away in 2008.

OPPOSITE:
Visitors
have many
opportunities
to enter the
"Powder Room"
in the Selkirks.

Selkirk Wilderness guests generally arrive in the sleepy town of Meadow Creek on Sundays. Here, two cats wait to spirit you to the lodge. For the rest of the week, you'll settle into a routine rife with powder. The operation has access to thirty square miles of terrain in the Selkirks and Purcells, more area than you'll find at Whistler and Vail combined. The region is blessed with an abundance of dry powder, an average of more than fifty feet a year; some have dubbed it the Powder Room. This is the result of a convenient convergence. The region's big lakes (Kootenay and Duncan) seed storms from the west as they meet the mountains to create abundant moisture; glaciers in the region help keep the snow nicely chilled. ("The powder is often so deep, you'll get to powder your nose, whether you like it or not!" Lyndell quipped.) Thanks to the Selkirk team's extensive network of cat paths, visitors can expect to cover between twelve thousand and eighteen thousand vertical feet a day through bowls, chutes, and glades—and an average of eighty thousand feet over the course of five days of skiing/boarding. Some runs pack a whopping four thousand vertical feet. Lyndell described a typical day:

"After a phenomenal breakfast, you head out in one of the cats for your first run. Some of the terrain is very close to the lodge, so you're in the snow in minutes. I find that there's an amazing variety of terrain with Selkirk Wilderness Skiing. Some places you go, every run seems the same. Here, every run is different. You'll ski tight trees on a slope with fairly moderate pitch, then you'll get a steeper run with the trees wider apart. I recall one run on a former avalanche path where the trees had been taken out. New trees had sprouted but they were still only really small. They looked like mini Christmas trees. You could really put the afterburners on, because if you hit a tree, it didn't matter . . . well, maybe it mattered to the tree! During the off-season, they do a bit of glading on some of the runs. The guides—many of whom have been with Selkirk Wilderness for ten years— go out and fell the trees themselves, and they know just what to take down to make for a great experience. The cats are very comfortable. In between runs, you can warm up a bit, listen to music, eat homemade brownies, and have a warm drink. It's very relaxing, though none of the rides are very long." (Selkirk still runs Bombardier cats, including one of 2010 vintage. In this model, seats face forward, there are drink holders, storage cupboards, and easy-to-navigate steps. The tracks are spiked to get you to fresh powder faster.)

"The dinners that the chefs create are amazing," Lyndell added. (Dishes include beef tenderloin with Yorkshire pudding, crab-filled Dover sole with charred tomato–basil tart, and cilantro mint chicken thighs with lemongrass Thai curry.) "The lodge is not quite as over-the-top as some cat- and heli-ski operations I've visited. But it's quite comfortable and very friendly. I'd say that the folks at Selkirk Wilderness have found a good middle path between utilitarian surroundings and opulence."

It's pleasant to return to the comfort of the Bombardier after your last run to warm up and swap stories en route to the lodge. But the folks at Selkirk Wilderness figure that you haven't come this far to take the easy route. So at the end of the day, the cat drops you off near the summit of Meadow Mountain so you can descend more than four thousand feet to the front porch of the lodge.

A warm fire, appetizers, and libations will be waiting.

LYNDELL "LUSCIOUS" KEATING is the chief editor of Powderhounds.com, a group of ski and snowboard enthusiasts who have traveled the world in search of the best powder stash. Based in Australia, Lyndell's hallmark is her pink Barbie helmet, which she hopes will help her retain youthful knees so she can ski powder into her seventies.

If You Go

▶ **Getting There:** Visitors from the United States can fly to Spokane, Washington, and drive the five hours to Meadow Creek, where a cat will pick you up. Spokane is served by several carriers, including Alaska Airlines (800-252-7522; www.alaskaair.com) and Delta Airlines (800-221-1212; www.delta.com).

▶ **Season:** Selkirk Wilderness Skiing generally operates from late December to mid-April. Mid-January through mid-March usually offers the best snow.

▶ **Lift Tickets:** Packages that include six nights of lodging and five days of cat skiing range from $2,580 to $4,800 (CAD), depending on the time of year. See details at www.selkirkwilderness.com.

▶ **Level of Difficulty:** You'll cover twelve thousand to eighteen thousand feet of vertical a day; Selkirk recommends you have at least intermediate powder skills.

DESTINATION 10

WHISTLER BLACKCOMB

RECOMMENDED BY **Andrew Weibrecht**

Andrew "Warhorse" Weibrecht arrived in British Columbia at Whistler Blackcomb in February 2010 with the goal of taking home a medal in the downhill or Super-G events. Instead, he got to ski . . . and ski, and ski.

"We'd arrived and gotten settled," he recalled, "and had a chance to do several training runs on the downhill course. We got ready to do the race, but it started snowing. It snowed all that night, and the next day, and the next. The racing kept getting postponed, and there was nothing left to do but to go powder skiing. Eventually the snow stopped enough to get the race off, but only after four or five days of freeskiing—some of the best day-after-day skiing I've ever had."

Incidentally, Andrew also achieved his initial objective, winning a bronze in the Super-G!

Whistler Blackcomb sits roughly seventy miles due north of Vancouver, in British Columbia's Coast Mountains. The two mountains rise vertiginously, climbing nearly a mile from the floor of Pemberton Valley to heights of 7,160 feet (Whistler) and 7,494 feet (Blackcomb). If there's a word to describe Whistler Blackcomb, it might be "vast." The resort—North America's largest—has a staggering 8,100 acres of terrain (including 1,100 acres of inbounds and out-of-bounds terrain and ninety-nine acres of terrain parks), two hundred marked trails (including two trails that stretch seven miles each), twelve bowls, an average snowfall of thirty feet, thirty-seven lifts (enough firepower to accommodate more than sixty thousand skiers/snowboarders an hour), and a mile of vertical drop.

And to think it all started with a humble fishing lodge!

The region was first recognized for its recreation potential by Alex and Myrtle Philip, two transplants from Maine, in 1911. By 1914, the Philips had established the Rainbow

OPPOSITE:
A boarder takes
flight from a
tabletop jump
at Whistler's
terrain park.

Lodge on the shores of Alta Lake; the lodge was named for the lake's resident rainbow trout. (The town was originally named Alta Lake, but took the name Whistler in recognition of the high-pitched calls of hoary marmots, a species of ground squirrel endemic to the surrounding mountains.) With the Pacific Great Eastern Railway in place to convey visitors to the lake's shores, the Rainbow Lodge soon became an acclaimed angling destination. By the 1920s, it was the most popular summer resort west of the Canadian Rockies. By 1960, plans were abreast to begin development of a ski resort in Whistler on London Mountain, in hopes of attracting the 1968 Olympics. Though that bid fell short, development continued, and the rechristened Whistler Mountain's four-person gondola began rolling in February 1966. With North America's greatest vertical, it was immediately on the map. When the adjoining Blackcomb Mountain opened in 1980, an alpine juggernaut was born. The two mountains operated independently until 1997, when they were officially merged. (Since 2008, the upper reaches of Whistler and Blackcomb have been connected by the PEAK 2 PEAK Gondola, an engineering marvel that conveys riders 2.5 miles at a height of more than 1,400 feet!)

And of course, Whistler Blackcomb was finally visited by the Winter Olympics and Paralympics . . . fifty years after the idea was initially hatched.

Whistler Blackcomb is known for its extensive intermediate terrain (more than 50 percent of the two mountains), with cruisers that seem to run forever. One favorite takes you nearly three miles down Blackcomb Glacier. Some of the terrain off the Harmony and Symphony quads will also prove inspiring to skiers/boarders of average ability; on a clear day, Highway 86 offers tremendous valley views. Want to enjoy your own Olympic moment? The Dave Murray Downhill is in the wheelhouse for intermediates, especially when it's groomed. For experts, there's something for everyone—big, beautiful bowls like Flute, Whistler, Ruby, and Sapphire; couloirs like Pakalolo and Extreme (once known as Saddam Couloir); and pretty much anything you can access from Spanky's Ladder. With such terrain, it's no wonder that Whistler Blackcomb has fostered many snow-sport heroes, including Eric Pehota, Shane Szocs, Ashleigh McIvor, and Steve Podborski.

Given its size and the number of visitors who make their way here (upwards of two million a season), it should come as no surprise that Whistler Village's après-ski amenities are as alluring as the resort's terrain. There are one hundred restaurants (give or take a few), ranging from pub grub to gastropub, to choose from, and some twenty bars and clubs. The village is pedestrian-only—a civilized touch typical of civilized British Columbia.

"I've skied at Whistler several times," Andrew continued, "and every time there's been great snow. The first time, I was there to participate in an international children's race, the Whistler Cup. I skied all day every day during that visit; racing took a backseat. The second time was in 2010. Storms roll in off the Pacific, and there's always fresh powder. The mountains rise so high and straight from sea level. There will be times when it may be too warm for good conditions on the bottom half of the mountains, but you know there will be great skiing at the top.

"One of my coaches used to be a ski instructor at Whistler, and when we were there for the Olympics, he had the skinny on the best spots to find fresh powder. Once something was skied out, we went elsewhere. At one point, we got up to a spot called Harmony Bowl. We were waiting in line, among the first thirty people to ski it that day. There was an awesome deep pitch and endless untracked snow. A high point of those freeskiing days was making big, high-speed powder turns all the way down that pitch."

ANDREW WEIBRECHT is sibling no. 4 in a family of five and took up skiing after he begged his parents to let him join older brother Jonathan at Whiteface. Now one of the most exhilarating ski racers to watch kick out of the start gate, he was the 2010 Olympic Super-G bronze medalist. When he's not on the slopes, Andrew enjoys fishing, golf, and mountain and road biking.

If You Go

▶ **Getting There:** Most visitors fly into Vancouver, which is served by most major carriers. From Vancouver, Whistler is a two-hour drive; bus and train transfers are available.

▶ **Season:** Whistler Blackcomb is generally open from late November through late April.

▶ **Lift Tickets:** Adult three-day passes begin at around $200 (CAD), depending on when you visit.

▶ **Level of Difficulty:** The largest ski area in North America, Whistler Blackcomb has terrain suited to skiers/boarders of all levels of ability.

▶ **Accommodations:** Whistler has a broad variety of lodging options; visit www.whistler blackcomb.com or call 866-218-9690 for details.

MAMMOTH MOUNTAIN

RECOMMENDED BY **Steve Taylor**

"There are so many attributes that make Mammoth a place skiers and boarders need to visit before they take off for the great hereafter," Steve Taylor, aka the Mammoth Snowman, enthused. "On any given day during the season, you'll be able to find some really good snow. On many mountains, that's not the case. I'm out there 120 to 150 days a year, and I always find some good snow. Another aspect of Mammoth that's unique is the wind. Wind is not always your friend on the mountain, but there are times when it works in your favor at Mammoth—it creates this phenomenon that we call "wind buff." The wind buff is this soft, powdery snow that coats the surface of the hill. It's incredible to ski on. Finally, Mammoth has one of the longest seasons of any resort anywhere. The management has a policy that they'll begin running chairs as soon as there's enough snow, even if it's just one section of the mountain. I have skied as early as the first week of October, and as late as August 16."

Mammoth Mountain is located along the eastern spine of the Sierra Nevada, just below the southeastern edge of Yosemite National Park. (The area is often associated with Southern California, as Southlanders make up the lion's share of its visitors. Most maps, however, place Mammoth in the northern half of the state; difficult mountain passes make for a long trip for Bay Area residents to reach Mammoth, so they tend to head for the Lake Tahoe region.) Mammoth is California's tallest ski area, with a top elevation of 11,053 feet, and one of the largest, with 3,500 acres of terrain. Yet the name comes not from its outsize proportions, but from its mining roots; one of the companies seeking gold there in the 1880s was the Mammoth Mining Company. The mountain has a volcanic provenance, and though the last eruption is believed to date back fifty thousand years, carbon dioxide still emits from fumaroles around the slopes.

OPPOSITE:
A skier takes
a jump at
Mammoth,
where the promise
of "wind buff"
snow awaits.

(In 2006, three ski patrol members perished, falling into a geothermal vent they were attempting to fence off. The resort monitors emissions from the mountains to help ensure visitor safety.)

Ski areas—at least in their conception—are often the inspiration of several committed individuals. No major area may be more associated with a single person than Mammoth with its founder, Dave McCoy. McCoy was an enthusiastic skier from El Segundo; he was California state champion in 1938. That same year, he began operating a rope tow on McGee Mountain, and by 1941, he'd obtained a roving permit for a portable rope tow. His favorite spot to take the tow was the north side of Mammoth. World War II interrupted McCoy's ambitions for Mammoth, but once the war concluded, he installed a permanent tow on the mountain, and conveyed skiers to the tow with several surplus army snow vehicles. McCoy eventually secured a permit from the U.S. Forest Service to further develop the mountain for winter recreation, and by 1955, he erected the first chairlift. Today, there are thirty-two lifts in total; McCoy, who is ninety-seven as of this writing, sold his interest in Mammoth for $365 million. "Dave McCoy really pioneered grooming methods," Steve continued. "He built a big service garage, and worked on answering the question 'How do you groom the snow so people can enjoy it?' Today, Mammoth has over thirty grooming machines, and they cover eight hundred to a thousand acres a night. Intermediate skiers and riders can find endless groomed runs, trails like Solitude, which is football-field wide."

Mammoth is known for its annual snowfall of four-hundred-plus inches and its extensive sunshine—three hundred days, on average. If Steve has it his way, he'd prefer to see snow falling when he rises. "If we get a day when it's snowing in the morning, I'll get my kids ready for school and drop them off," he said. "Next I'll grab a bagel and coffee at Stellar Brew & Deli, and head to the mountain. I want to be in the lift line at Little Eagle fifteen minutes before it opens. If it's snowing hard enough, they might close the upper mountain, but Lincoln Mountain, which is served by Little Eagle, stays open, as it's lower and heavily treed. You can run laps there until the winds are above seventy-five miles per hour. If the upper mountain is open and you're an advanced skier, you want to make sure you get to the top of the Panorama Gondola and Chair 23 and check out Climax, the Dropout, and Wipeout Chutes and Paranoid Flats. There are a few days a year when we'll see a couple of feet of snow during the day. When it's snowing three or four inches an hour, you get the sensation that the powder is accumulating faster than you can track it out. A lot of the more casual skiers stay inside, so you have endless fresh powder. People not used to the wind might be discouraged by it, but I encourage people to just put on an extra layer and a face mask and head out."

Given its relative proximity to Los Angeles and the Southland's surf and skateboard culture, it's not surprising that Mammoth has emerged as a favorite destination for snowboarders. The area features eight terrain parks that include the eighteen-foot Super Pipe and the twenty-two-foot Super-Duper Pipe. (Many snowboarding champions, including Shaun White, are frequent visitors.) "In the time I've been skiing, I've seen the progression of Mammoth as a freestyle and boarder destination," Steve described. "It's consistently rated among the top terrain park experiences. The snowboarder theme at Mammoth is defined by the Peanut Butter Rail Jam, which is held each spring. I've seen four thousand or five thousand people packed into the event." (Sponsored by the sport-clothing manufacturer Volcom, the Peanut Butter Rail Jam is an amateur snowboard contest where contestants can perform a series of tricks on rails and other apparatus. Win or lose, participants receive peanut butter and jelly sandwiches.)

"I remember driving up to the mountain one morning," Steve recalled. "It had snowed three or four feet the night before, really cold, Utah-style powder. I was pretty excited. I put on the radio, and the U2 song 'Beautiful Day' came on. [If you're not familiar with the song, the chorus goes 'It's a beau-ti-ful day!'] I got chills on my arms. I got to Canyon Lodge early that day, and was on the very first chair—Chair 22. I came off the chair, and was the first person coming down a trail called Viva. You're in view of everyone coming up Chair 22 when you're at the top of Viva. I was hearing the U2 song in my head, and when I made my first turn, the folks on the chairlift gave a loud 'Woo-hoo!' and I called back.

"When I got home, my daughter said, 'You know, your pocket called me today. I could hear you screaming "Woo-hoo!" '

"Incidentally, it was a bluebird, sunny day."

STEVE TAYLOR began skiing at Mammoth Mountain in 1969, and made the move north from Los Angeles in 1990 to be closer to the slopes. He started his first Internet Blog Reports in the summer of 1990 on Mammoth's first BBS system, and today regularly broadcasts snow reports and video footage on www.mammothsnowman.com. "I started the website because I wanted to get skiers from the Los Angeles area excited about coming up so I wouldn't have to ski alone," Steve explained. "Now I have twenty thousand new friends, thanks to the site." Steve still skis a hundred-plus times a year, and runs a local advertising agency, Steve Taylor Marketing (www.stevetaylormarketing.com).

If You Go

▶ **Getting There:** Mammoth is roughly three hundred miles from Los Angeles. The airport is served by both Alaska Airlines (800-252-7522; www.alaskaair.com) and United Airlines (800-864-8331; www.united.com).

▶ **Season:** Mammoth enjoys one of skiing's longest seasons, running from November to July; in 1994/95, the season went from October 8 through August 13.

▶ **Lift Tickets:** Adult day tickets are $96; multi-day tickets are available.

▶ **Level of Difficulty:** Mammoth's 150 trails offer a variety of terrain, classified as follows: 25 percent beginner; 40 percent intermediate; 15 percent expert; 20 percent advanced.

▶ **Accommodations:** There's a variety of lodging options in Mammoth Lakes, on the mountain and off. Mammoth Mountain Ski Area (800-MAMMOTH; www.mammoth mountain.com) provides an overview.

DESTINATION 12

SQUAW VALLEY USA

RECOMMENDED BY **Jonny Moseley**

Though he's skied just about everywhere worth skiing, Jonny Moseley feels that Squaw Valley is in his blood.

"My dad grew up on the San Francisco Peninsula," he explained, "and didn't get to ski much as a kid. But in the little skiing he did, he took to it. When he was able to drive, or had friends who could, he'd rally up to Sugar Bowl—mainly because it was closer than Squaw to the Bay Area. It was another hour to get to Squaw at that time, on a tough road. Squaw wasn't a great option until the highway [I-80] was built. Around 1970, my dad moved to Puerto Rico. He met my mom, and my two brothers and I were born there. Eventually he moved back to Marin County, California. He really missed skiing, and he thought it would be a great thing for his boys. So he started loading us into the car and making the trip to Squaw. He put us boys in a kid's ski program. My first coach was a woman named Linda. She taught me how to ski.

"Later, after I made the U.S. Ski Team, I got to ski all around the world. Once I won in the Olympics (1998), I worked at a few other big resorts. Still, I always longed to get back to Squaw. I've often thought about why, and it's tough to explain. It's not the highest mountain, it doesn't have the most snow, and it can have some extreme conditions, which can be trying. When conditions are good, it's just an incredible place to ski. When conditions aren't right, it can be pretty bad. But still, there's an essence about it. Part of it probably comes from having grown up there. I know the nooks and crannies so well, and it's hard to get that same experience somewhere else."

Squaw Valley rests between the towns of Truckee and Tahoe City, in the northern Lake Tahoe area; from some of Squaw's higher peaks, you can spy the lake, renowned for its sparkling blue water. Squaw first opened in 1949, with a single chairlift. Thanks to the

13

DESTINATION

persuasive powers of cofounder (and longtime chairman) Alex Cushing during a presentation before the International Olympic Committee in 1955, Squaw was able to secure the 1960 Olympics, despite its lack of infrastructure. Squaw Valley USA rose to the occasion, and the facilities were completed in time. Cushing's timing was ideal, as the 1960 Winter Olympics were the first winter games that were televised, showcasing Lake Tahoe as a winter destination and boosting the overall visibility of skiing. (Though the Olympics brought the first major international ski competition to Squaw Valley, records show that miners drawn to the region in search of gold held ski races as early as the 1860s.) Today, Squaw's terrain extends across six peaks and four thousand acres, with 2,850 feet of vertical drop.

Any discussion of Squaw Valley will eventually shift to KT-22 and its environs—"the Mothership," in local parlance. Jonny Moseley has the distinction of having a run named in his honor off KT-22, though not all the regulars were happy about that. "There are lots of hard-core skiers at Squaw, and KT-22 is their territory," Jonny continued. "One survey rated Squaw the second most hostile place for visitors to ski. I think that's a badge of pride for some folks. When they named the run for me, some people were pissed off, as it was a hard-core local run with sustained moguls. I think my favorite run off the Mothership is Chute 75. It's the kind of chute you'd normally have to hike to at other mountains, but here it's right off the lift. You can start skiing Chute 75 when you're eight and continue to age eighty. Sometimes it's powdery, sometimes icy, sometimes there are moguls. It's always different in there.

"I remember being up at the top of KT-22 toward the end of the day, and there were some local guys hanging out, waiting for the chair to close. The sun was starting to go down, and I asked what they were waiting for. It turned out they were waiting for everyone to ski down so they could side-flip Chute 75 so it would be sweet for the next morning. That sums up the special atmosphere at Squaw. It's because of such devotion that I choose to make it my home mountain."

Some of Jonny's favorite experiences at Squaw might be beyond the skill/nerve level that most of us can muster. But a few are more accessible, like the morning patrol. "A few years back, I was doing a Warren Miller film up at Squaw," Jonny recalled. "They took us up to the top of Emigrant Peak in a cat, and we watched the sun come up. Then we made fresh tracks on Funnel and Silverado. Granted, that's not everyone's typical day. But now, conditions permitting, you can do an early up on Shirley and/or Granite for an extra $25.

OPPOSITE:
Dawn light
falls upon the
Palisades after
a five-foot dump.

DESTINATION

13

The tram leaves at 7:30 and gets you up to the top ahead of the crowds. You forget what it's like to be up there with no people. If it has snowed overnight, there will probably be a foot of snow. You'll want to use rocker skis, which Shane McConkey revolutionized for the powder at Squaw. Another thing visitors should do while visiting Squaw is pick up a copy of *Squallywood* [a guide/coffee-table book by Dr. Robb Gaffney], which details all of the area's history and its most famous runs. You can find exactly where Women's Olympics Downhill was held, locate the Men's Giant Slalom Run, and see the lines taken by some of Squaw's most notorious extreme skiers in your favorite ski movies. Even if you don't want to try to ski these lines, it's cool to ski to them."

One of Squaw's little endearments is found at Wildflour, perhaps the area's most renowned bakery. "Wildflour is in the old Olympic Plaza House," Jonny said. "They make great cookies, cinnamon rolls, now sandwiches as well. The woman who owns Wildflour offers Squaw regulars who win a gold medal in the Olympics a 'lifetime cookie pass'— that is, you get free cookies for life. If you win a silver medal, you get free cookies for a year; if you win a bronze, you don't get anything. There's a wall with photos of the winners from Squaw. I got a lifetime cookie pass after Nagano. All the kids know that if they win a gold medal, they get the lifetime pass. Most kids that stop to talk to me skip right past my gold medal. They want to know if I really got a lifetime cookie pass."

No day at Squaw is quite complete without a stop at Le Chamois. "The loft bar captures all the history of Squaw," Jonny added. "It's the locals' bar. An April Fools' e-mail went out earlier this year saying that Chamois would have to close down. It was not well received at all."

JONNY MOSELEY was born in San Juan, Puerto Rico, in 1975, and hit the snow for the first time when his family relocated to the San Francisco Bay Area in 1978. In 1993, he was selected to the U.S. Ski Team and, after narrowly missing a spot on the 1994 Olympic team, began preparing himself for the 1998 Olympic Games. In 1997, Jonny put school on hold and became a full-time skier for the first time in his life. He won the first two World Cup events of the 1997/98 season, and secured a spot on the U.S. Olympic team. Jonny arrived in Nagano, Japan, in February 1998, and one week later, he won the first American gold medal of the Games with what had become his signature move, the 360-degree mute-grab. He returned to the World Cup, winning the last two events of the season and securing the 1998 World Cup mogul skiing title as well as the U.S. National title with nine wins on the season. The U.S. Olympic Committee named him Sportsman of the Year. After his Olympic win, Jonny looked beyond the World Cup circuit to round out his skills as a skier. He entered ESPN's X Games and took second place with his newly developed trick, the Dinner Roll. He trademarked the Jonny Moseley SKI logo, co-branded product lines with several of his sponsors, developed a video game, and hosted *Snow Zone with Jonny Moseley* for Fox Sports Net. In 2006, Jonny achieved another of his goals, graduating from UC Berkeley. In 2007, he was inducted into the U.S. National Ski Hall of Fame and became the narrator of the Warren Miller ski films. Today, Jonny hosts a weekly radio show on Sirius Satellite Radio, continues his TV work, and is chief mountain host at Squaw Valley USA. He is also an avid sailor, surfer, and golfer.

If You Go

▶ **Getting There:** Squaw Valley is roughly an hour drive from Reno, Nevada, and a two-hour drive from Sacramento; both cities are served by many carriers.

▶ **Season:** Squaw generally opens on Thanksgiving and remains in operation through the end of April.

▶ **Lift Tickets:** Day passes begin at $84.

▶ **Level of Difficulty:** Squaw offers terrain for everyone. Roughly 25 percent is rated beginner terrain; 45 percent intermediate; and 30 percent expert.

▶ **Accommodations:** Lodging options in the Village at Squaw Valley and around Lake Tahoe are highlighted at www.squaw.com.

13

DESTINATION

PORTILLO

RECOMMENDED BY **Greg Harms**

"I first went down to Portillo in 1990," began longtime instructor and powder guide Greg Harms. "The director of the ski school at Heavenly [in Lake Tahoe] asked if I wanted to go to Chile to be an instructor. I wouldn't have to pay for anything, he said, and I'd only have to teach three hours a day. I was twenty, and hadn't been out of the country beyond Tijuana, so I said, 'Of course!' I fell in love with Portillo immediately—the big yellow hotel, the amphitheater setting in the Andes, and the people. There's a certain magic about Portillo, a welcoming vibe. The feeling there encourages you to be open and meet new people who share your passion. It oozes skiing."

Portillo ("Little Pass" in Spanish) rests one hundred miles northeast of Santiago, near the border of Chile and Argentina at Paso Los Libertadores. The site of the resort, on the banks of Laguna del Inca at an elevation of 9,400 feet, was first explored as a ski venue in the early 1930s. Word slowly spread, and alpinists from abroad began venturing south. By 1949, a resort with several lifts and a hotel had opened, though Portillo did not begin to come into its own until the early 1960s, when it was acquired by two Americans, Bob Purcell and Dick Aldrich. The area gained international recognition when the Alpine World Ski Championships were held there in 1966—the first and only World Cup event held in South America. Plans to stage the event at Portillo were nearly quashed when a tremendous storm and subsequent avalanche obliterated all but two of the resort's chairlifts. Working with the lift manufacturer Poma and various avalanche experts, the area's lifts were reimagined, and completed in time for the competition. This reconstruction inspired Portillo's trademark *va et vient* lifts (more on that later).

"It's a little hectic when you first arrive at Portillo," Greg continued, "as it's a Saturday-to-Saturday program. When I'm guiding, I call it 'Hugs and High Fives'—I'm giving

OPPOSITE:
The famous
yellow lodge
at Portillo,
one of South
America's most
storied resorts.

hugs to the group that's leaving and high-fiving the folks that are coming in. [There are a total of four hundred guests each week.] The folks at Portillo call guests *passajeros* [passsengers], as once you arrive, it's like you're on a ship; we're all on our own on an ocean of snow. The hotel is a classic structure; it's bombproof, and with good reason—storms here can be massive. There is something like 450 employees, and many have been there forever. Jaime, the bartender in the Bar Central, has been there for thirty-five years; Juan, the maître d', has been on staff for twenty-five years. Over my twenty years, I've gotten to know more than two hundred of the employees. You go there the first time as a stranger. When you come back, the employees all remember you."

The warmth of Portillo's atmosphere helps make for a memorable stay. But the primary reason that people make the long trek south is the quality of the terrain. The mountain averages some three hundred inches of snow a year; while you can't always count on deep powder, the region enjoys many clear, sunny days—not a bad trade-off. There are a number of long, well-groomed trails for intermediate skiers, though it's the two-thousand-plus acres of off-piste terrain that have captivated Greg for two decades. "The surface lifts at Portillo open up a huge chunk of expert terrain," he said. "At the end of the day, that's why I love it. The steeps, chutes, cliffs, and couloirs—I couldn't have imagined a better place to freeski. And there just aren't many people.

"A quintessential part of the Portillo experience is riding the *va et vient*—'come and go'—surface lifts, which you find on the resort's steepest runs: Condor, Roca Jack, Las Viachas, and El Cara Cara. These pulley lifts take you to the classic black diamond/double black diamond terrain. Since they're in avalanche paths, key parts of the lift, like the motor, can be taken off during big snow years, and reassembled when avalanche danger has passed. You stand side by side, up to five people at a time, and it pulls you up. You have to get off one at a time. On the Roca Jack 'come and go,' the lift stops on a thirty-seven-degree slope. If you fall, you'll wipe out the other people."

There is no shortage of world-class lines at Portillo. One is the Lake Run off the Condor lift, a broad slope that plummets through a series of gullies and boulder-dotted ridges . . . though some would say that the real adventure unfolds on the traverse back to the lift or the hotel. "Some years ago, the Purcells blasted a little trail along the edge of a cliff," Greg explained. "It's no wider than the length of your skis, and the lake sits down below. You have to sidestep your way along the trail. It can be windy. Some people do the traverse and say, 'I never want to do that again!' Others just love the whole experience.

One of the other classic runs at Portillo—and in all the Southern Hemisphere—is the resort's biggest couloir, the Super C." Leaving the Roca Jack Poma, there's a climb that can take up to a half day (depending on the snow). On the way, you're treated to stunning views of a dozen mountain peaks flirting with twenty thousand feet, including Aconcagua, which is the largest mountain outside of the Himalayas. If you make it to the top, you're rewarded to a swooning descent of 4,300 vertical feet!

GREG HARMS has been guiding and teaching skiing in big-mountain environments since 1990. He is a fully certified PSIA ski and snowboard instructor, Level III avalanche forecaster, EMT, and fluent Spanish speaker. It is evident to anyone who skis with Greg that he absolutely loves his work. His first priority is your safety, and his second is that you enjoy your vacation immensely. He challenged himself to see if he could heli-ski for twenty-four continuous hours and finished the day with more than one hundred thousand vertical feet. He spends more than 280 days a year on the snow all over the globe, much of that in the backcountry. Greg is currently a lead guide with the Tordrillo Mountain Lodge, managing more than 1.2 million acres of terrain, and operates Third Edge Heli (www.thirdedgeheli.com), which leads skiers/snowboarders on personalized heli-ski adventures in Alaska, Canada, and Chile. In his off-time, Greg enjoys surfing and warming his feet in the tropical locations of the world.

If You Go

▶ **Getting There:** Portillo is roughly a hundred miles from Santiago, which is served by many major carriers.

▶ **Season:** Late June through early October

▶ **Lift Tickets:** All inclusive rates (seven nights' lodging, four meals per day, lift tickets, etc.) range from $1,790 to $4,000 per person (based on double occupancy), depending on the season. Visit www.skiportillo.com for details.

▶ **Level of Difficulty:** While there's some good groomed terrain for intermediate skiers/boarders, much of the terrain is geared toward advanced skiers.

▶ **Accommodations:** You have one option for lodging at Portillo: Grand Hotel Portillo (www.skiportillo.com).

ARAPAHOE BASIN

RECOMMENDED BY **Candace Horgan**

It was on a drive back from another ski resort that Candace Horgan discovered Arapahoe Basin. "When I graduated from college on the East Coast, I wanted to be a ski bum out west," she said. "But by the time I made my way out to Colorado, I had quit skiing. My skiing in the Northeast had come to feel like a merry-go-round. The goal was to track runs, and I'd go up and down as fast as I could. I'd taken up ice climbing in lieu of skiing, and was getting out sixty to seventy days a year. I happened to go to Winter Park one day and saw a friend telemarking. It was so graceful, like she was dancing. I tried it and quickly fell in love, and got a pass at Winter Park.

"I was still doing some ice climbing, and I went over to Vail to climb. On the way back home, I was driving over Loveland Pass. As I'm winding along, I looked up, and there was the Pallavicini Face at A-Basin (what regulars call Arapahoe)—wide-open, steep, and grand. The higher up I drove on the pass, the more intimidating it looked. I wanted to try it, and soon I did. I skied all the runs off of the Pallavicini lift, many of the tree runs. I liked the intimacy of the place and the high-alpine feel, which seems a little more wild than many of the Colorado areas. I was instantly drawn to it. I came back later in the season and skied the trails off the East Wall. The next season, I got a pass at A-Basin."

Summit County, an hour and change west of Denver along the I-70 corridor, is not devoid of ski areas. The region is home to Keystone, Breckenridge, and Copper Mountain; Vail and Beaver Creek are nearby. Though A-Basin sits among a number of big-name neighbors, there are several characteristics that set it apart, as Candace described. "First, it's the highest resort in Colorado, with a base elevation of 10,780 feet, and a summit—with a little hiking—more than 13,000 feet. This gives A-Basin one of the longest seasons of any resort in the United States. Some years, you can begin skiing in mid-October, and

OPPOSITE:
A-Basin's base elevation of nearly 11,000 feet gives it one of Colorado's longest ski seasons.

continue until late June. This creates a unique spring skiing scene. There's a parking area right at the lift, and in the spring they call it 'the Beach.' People will pull out barbecues, take a few runs, hang out in the parking lot, play Frisbee. It's like a tailgate party. There aren't any condos at the base of the mountain, no lodging on premises at all. That gives A-Basin an old-school feel. Because the area is so high, there's a lot of old-style intermediate terrain. Much of the upper half of the mountain is wide-open blue terrain. Less-seasoned skiers can get that big-mountain, high-alpine experience, instead of being stuck on the lower half of the mountain." (This big-mountain experience is enhanced by the proximity of several peaks eclipsing thirteen thousand and fourteen thousand feet.)

Arapahoe Basin has been in operation since 1946, though today's area is a far cry from the single tow rope operation that Larry Jump, Max and Edna Dercum, and a handful of other proponents established. (The tow went from midmountain to the top; the first season's 1,200 skiers were conveyed to the tow rope in an army weapons carrier; a lift was installed the following year.)

In 2008, A-Basin saw its terrain nearly double (to nine hundred acres) with the opening of the Montezuma Bowl on the backside. "When Montezuma opened, it took a lot of pressure off Pali," Candace added. "It's a high-alpine bowl on the west side with cornices where you might have to drop as far as fifteen feet. On the east side, there are blue cruisers, much mellower than the west." The area's 108 trails see an average of 350 inches of snow a year; snowmaking on select trails abets the long season.

Pallavicini (or Pali, as it's affectionately called) is A-Basin's marquee run, though many would call it a headwall rather than a run. (Pali takes its name from the Pallavicini Couloir on Grossglockner, which is Austria's highest peak at 12,457 feet.) Pali Face—and for that matter, the other trails off the Pallavicini lift—are all double black diamond, with pitches approaching forty degrees. Monstrous moguls face you on the left side of the face; a copse of trees marks the right—choose your poison! "On a day when I'm not ski patrolling, I like to get in one intermediate run to warm up and then start running laps on Pali," Candace said. "I'll take main face first, which has the steepest drop, and then go to a run called the Spine. There's usually some great snow in there. If Upper International were open, I'd head over there next. It's a little run that skirts a cliff. I'd ride up Pali again and go over to the trees on the right. There are some nice chutes in the trees, called the Alleys [Upper, Lower, and West], and Gauthier, which has a steeper drop than the Alleys. Pali has lots of little places where you can find great terrain."

A-Basin has not one, but two iconic areas, the second being the East Wall. "It's all hike-in terrain," Candace said. "Depending on your line, it's twenty to forty-five minutes. It's very steep, but it looks worse than it actually is. One of the runs up there is called North Pole. At the top, you feel like how I imagine it would feel to be in the Alps. My favorite run on the East Wall is called Snorkel Nose. It's accessed by a forty-minute hike up from the top of Willy's Wide [a precarious run in itself]. There's a forty-degree drop at the top, but it soon opens up, and usually has great snow. With all the traversing you need to do on the East Wall, you might only get in five runs a day over there. But it's worth it."

CANDACE HORGAN is the communications director for the National Ski Patrol. A patroller at Arapahoe Basin since 2008, she attended the National Avalanche School in 2011 and 2012. She competed on the Extreme Telemark Tour in 2011, and has done some ski mountaineering in Colorado.

If You Go

▶ **Getting There:** A-Basin is ninety-six miles from the Denver airport, which is served by most major carriers.

▶ **Season:** A-Basin has a long season, beginning in October and, in many years, extending into June.

▶ **Lift Tickets:** Day tickets at A-Basin (888-272-7246; www.arapahoebasin.com) begin at $79.

▶ **Level of Difficulty:** A-Basin is known for its expert terrain but has plenty for less-seasoned skiers. Terrain is classified as 10 percent beginner; 30 percent intermediate; 37 percent advanced; and 23 percent expert.

▶ **Accommodations:** There's no on-site lodging at A-Basin, though there are many options within a five- to fifteen-mile radius. The area lists lodging partners at www.arapahoebasin.com.

ASPEN

RECOMMENDED BY **Chris Klug**

"As a twenty-year professional snowboarder and Olympic medalist, I've had the unique opportunity of traveling the world on my snowboard," Chris Klug declared. "I've ridden powder all over North America, Europe, South America, and Asia. I believe there's no place like Aspen. We've got four large resorts in one place—this doesn't exist elsewhere in North America. There's incredible ski and snowboard acreage, from intermediate family-friendly terrain to black diamond X Games stuff, and everything in between. You combine all this with the cultural and culinary opportunities that Aspen has to offer and you have something very special. I've never seen such big-city attractions in such a small town like Aspen—there's so many fun things to do on and off the mountain. While you often only hear about all the rich and famous people that spend time in Aspen, it's actually a very laid-back, down-to-earth town. I think many of our visitors come to Aspen to escape the spotlight and rat race to relax and enjoy many of the same activities Aspenites are so passionate about. Most of the locals respect that."

Though the nascent Aspen Ski Club cut a course on Aspen Mountain (which was served by massive sleds pulled up by an old mine hoist) in 1937, it would not be until after World War II that development would take hold. The war effort temporarily delayed Aspen's development, but in the long run it fostered the resort. An Austrian named Friedl Pfeifer was training with the army's 10th Mountain Division at Camp Hale, and became enamored with Aspen and its potential as a ski mecca through the aforementioned sled lift. After the war, he enlisted the support of a wealthy Chicagoan named Walter Paepcke, who hoped to build a cultural center in the mountains. They both got their wish. What was then the world's longest ski lift opened in 1947; in 1949, the Goethe Bicentennial was held in Aspen. The other mountains—Buttermilk, Highlands,

OPPOSITE:
Aspen is not
one resort but
four, including
Aspen Highlands
(shown here).

and Snowmass—came online over the next twenty years, and Aspen's prosperity (and élan) were cemented.

Chris shared his ideal itinerary if he only had two days at Aspen. "I'd spend one day on Aspen Mountain and one day at Highlands. On day one, I might begin with a big breakfast at Poppycock's Café, known for its oatmeal buttermilk pancakes. Then we'd walk across the street to Gondola Plaza and the Silver Queen lift, which zips you 3,267 vertical feet over 2.5 miles to the summit of Aspen Mountain [11,215 feet] in fifteen minutes. Now that I have a day job and a family, sometimes it's hard to get out and ride all day. With the Silver Queen right in town and the lift's speed, I can easily go out and do four or five laps in a couple hours. I'd do a bunch of laps off Silver Queen. If it's a good powder day, I'd head over to ride 'the Dumps' [e.g., Short Snort, Zaugg Dump, Last Dollar, and Perry's]. I might also ride off of Ruthie's lift. There were a number of mines on this part of the mountain, and you actually can ride through some of the old tailings and even over mine shafts. This area really collects the powder, and you can sometimes find soft snow here a week after the last storm. If I want to hit some gladed terrain, I like Jackpot and Bingo. When the boarding is done, I like the après scene right at the bottom of the mountain. The Ajax Tavern has fun people-watching—if you want to see some Wookie boots and fur, this is the place.

"On day two, it's on to Aspen Highlands. I think the most unique experience at Highlands—maybe at all of Aspen—is a trip up to Highlands Bowl. From the top of the Loge Peak lift, it's another seven hundred vertical feet up—about a thirty-minute hike. From the top, you have an amazing view out over some of my favorite 14ers—Maroon Peak [14,156 feet], Capitol [14,130 feet], and Pyramid [14,018 feet]. The Bowl itself gives you a 2,500-foot descent through what can be some phenomenal terrain. In some places, it's a forty-five-degree [or more] pitch, but there are some easier ways down. I have an uncle and cousin from Pennsylvania that I brought up there some years back. Even though they weren't acclimatized to the elevation, they were able to do it. They still talk about it today. It's a world-class backcountry experience without really leaving the resort."

There's a thrill to be had in riding Highlands Bowl or the Dumps. But Chris finds a quieter kind of satisfaction in the huts that dot the Rockies around Aspen. "Three to five times each winter, I'll head off to one of the huts that are spread from Aspen to Leadville, Crested Butte, and Vail. [The thirty huts, connected by 350 miles of suggested routes, are managed by the 10th Mountain Division Hut Association.] You just take a sleeping bag and food; most of the huts have heat and light. It's great to escape for a night, to be beyond cell phones and tablets."

CHRIS KLUG learned to ski at an early age, and at nine years old began snowboarding in Moon Boots, with the flex determined by the number of wraps of duct tape. His snowboarding accomplishments include three-time Winter Olympian, bronze medalist in Salt Lake City in 2002, eleven-time U.S. National Champion, twenty-year veteran of the Snowboard World Cup, and five-time World Cup Champion. Chris has spent plenty of time exploring mountain communities around the world and believes the best one is situated in the Elk Mountains in Aspen, Colorado. In addition to his passion for outdoor activities, Chris devotes his energy to promoting lifesaving organ and tissue donation through the Chris Klug Foundation (www.chrisklugfoundation.org). As a twelve-year liver transplant recipient himself, Chris is dedicated to giving back to help the more than one hundred thousand people waiting across the country for a second chance at life. Chris is proud to be a licensed real estate broker with Aspen Snowmass Sotheby's International Realty in Aspen, Colorado.

If You Go

▶ **Getting There:** Direct air service to Aspen is available from United Airlines (800-864-8331; www.united.com). It's a 220-mile drive from Denver to Aspen.

▶ **Season:** The four areas at Aspen open between Thanksgiving and early December, and close for the season in mid-April.

▶ **Lift Tickets:** Two-day lift tickets in prime season begin at $196. Multi-day packages are available; visit www.aspensnowmass.com for details. Your lift ticket gives you access to all four mountains.

▶ **Level of Difficulty:** Between Aspen, Aspen Highlands, Snowmass, and Buttermilk, there's something for everyone—including an extensive, X Game–worthy terrain park.

▶ **Accommodations:** Aspen Snowmass (800-525-6200; www.aspensnowmass.com) lists the many lodging options available in town.

16
DESTINATION

CRESTED BUTTE

RECOMMENDED BY **Derek Taylor**

Many a high school student in the eastern United States dreams of aligning their skiing plans—I mean, academic futures—with a program of study in the Mountain West. Most resign themselves to a leafy quadrangle around Boston, or if they're lucky, a campus near the Adirondacks or Green Mountains. Once Derek Taylor made the break, he never looked back.

"I grew up outside Hartford, Connecticut, and did my first two years of college as a business major playing soccer for Roger Williams University in Rhode Island," he began. "For my junior year, I transferred to Western State College of Colorado in Gunnison. I wasn't counting on staying more than a year, but things worked out differently. The unofficial motto of the school is 'Get a degree while you ski!' I did just that. I switched to an English major, and took classes Monday, Wednesday, Friday. Tuesday and Thursday were ski days up the road at Mount Crested Butte. By senior year I had moved up to the Butte, and was coming back into Gunnison two days a week to finish up my course work. People would ask me, 'What are you going to do with an English degree?' My response generally was 'I don't know, write for a ski magazine.' I ended up staying in Crested Butte for eleven years, and eventually began working for *Powder* magazine. I sometimes see friends from my college days, and they comment that I'm the only one of our classmates who's doing what I said I was going to do. But it wasn't due to good planning as much as just a product of being in the Butte."

Crested Butte—the town and the ski mountain—sits in the Elk Mountain range, in west-central Colorado. As the crow flies, Mount Crested Butte is less than thirty miles from Aspen, though in general ambience, it's much further removed. Much of the Butte's past glory as a prosperous mining center has been preserved, though now its Victorian-

OPPOSITE:
The mountain at Crested Butte— like the town's residents—are known for their toughness.

DESTINATION 17

era structures are more likely to house fine restaurants and cozy inns than general stores. Still, the town has maintained an edge. "Crested Butte is literally and figuratively at the end of the road," Derek continued. "The people it attracts are independent-minded, a little quirky, and a lot tough. For a town its size, it attracts a lot of smart and talented people, people who are there because they love the small-town feeling. A lot of people want to be able to ski in and ski out, and you do have that option at the mountain. But when I visit, I like to be in town. The restaurants and nightlife are there, and it's close by; you can jump on an 8:15 bus and be in line with everyone who stayed at the mountain."

Like its people, Mount Crested Butte is tough, touted as one of the steepest, most technical areas in the United States. The mountain takes its name from its domed or cresting peak; it's actually a laccolith, a volcanic formation that stands alone in the Gunnison Valley, unconnected to other hills by a range or ridgeline. It became known as the original epicenter of extreme skiing in 1992 when it was the first resort to sanction an extreme competition. "There's a lot of craggy, tree-filled terrain," Derek said. "It can be very technical, and there's not always the best snow. People who ski here with any frequency learn to set an edge and turn quickly. At Crested Butte, you need to take a smart approach to how you attack the mountain, an approach you might not need to take at a place like Alta. You need to be on your game. On a good snow day, I like to get on the Silver Queen lift, and then take the T-bar (called the High Lift) on up to the Headwall. I'll take one of the Headwall chutes down to the North Face lift, ski down to Paradise, and keep that rotation going."

Though Crested Butte is celebrated for its edgy terrain, there's a good deal of intermediate skiing among the mountain's 1,058 acres. A nice collection of blue trails resides in Paradise Bowl, right below the Headwall.

Early spring is a special time at Crested Butte. The hill's cylindrical shape and the layout of its terrain provides 270 degrees of exposure, which can make for first-rate spring skiing/boarding throughout the day. "When you head up to the mountain, it's frozen," Derek said, "but if you begin at Third Bowl, off the North Face lift, and then follow the sun, you'll have great snow as the day progresses. Something about the spring skiing attracts lots of people from other mountains. When I was living there, you could always make new friends and extend your network."

Though it's still home to the National Extreme Skiing and Snowboarding Championships, there's another event that holds a special spot in the hearts of Crested

Butte regulars: the Al Johnson Memorial Uphill/Downhill Telemark Ski Race. Named for a mailman who delivered mail on skis to remote mining camps around Crested Butte, the race requires participants to make their way six hundred vertical feet from the North Face lift to the summit of North Face and then ski down several double black diamond runs— Hard Slab, Old Pro, Last Steep, and Black Eagle Run—to the finish. Costumes are encouraged. "The Uphill/Downhill brings out a strange mix of folks," Derek recalled. "You have some world-class cross-country skiers and people in outlandish costumes; one year, a skier was dressed as a giant penis named Al's Johnson.

"There used to be a Club Med in Crested Butte. The resort and their clientele didn't really fit in that well with the local crowd. One year, I participated in a team race where we dressed as Club Medders. Someone got ahold of some of their bibs, and we skied right behind each other, the way their instructors did their lessons. We didn't do very well in the race, but we had lots of fun."

DEREK TAYLOR was the editor of *Powder* magazine for five years and is currently the founding editor of www.mtnadvisor.com. He grew up on the East Coast during the long-ski era, and spent a decade in and around Crested Butte. He doesn't mind wiggling into tighter lines for fresher snow. He likes it all, but is happiest in the trees on a storm day. He refuses to accept that the Whalers ever left Hartford. Not afraid to rock a mullet or a perm.

If You Go

► **Getting There:** The town of Crested Butte is served by United Airlines (800-864-8331; www.united.com) via Denver.

► **Season:** Crested Butte is open from late November through early April.

► **Lift Tickets:** Adult day tickets are $59; multi-day tickets are available. Get more information at the Crested Butte website (www.skicb.com).

► **Level of Difficulty:** 80 percent of the mountain is rated as intermediate-friendly, though the advanced terrain is very advanced.

► **Accommodations:** Derek likes to stay at Elk Mountain Lodge (800-374-6521; www.elkmountainlodge.com). Other options are listed at the Crested Butte website (www.skicb.com/cbmr/lodging.aspx).

17

DESTINATION

SILVERTON MOUNTAIN

RECOMMENDED BY **Cory Smith**

Silverton Mountain was established in 2002 with an unofficial motto: "More Powder to the People!" Professional snowboarder and videographer Cory Smith spent his formative years in Silverton, though it would be later in life before he'd experience the mountain in all its glory.

"When I was growing up, there was no chair," Cory began. "I started skiing and then snowboarding at Purgatory, down the road from Silverton toward Durango. Sometimes we'd hike up on the lower sections of the hill that would become Silverton Mountain and play around. Even then, you could see the potential of the terrain. I remember wishing that there was a lift."

Like many Colorado mountain towns, Silverton started life as a mining center in the San Juan Mountains near the southwestern corner of the state. It sits at 9,305 feet, and rests in the shadow of several 14ers. Silverton's mining days are in its past; it may be best known as the terminus of the Durango and Silverton Narrow Gauge Railroad, a National Historic Landmark and tourist favorite. In 1999, Aaron Brill set out to change that. After visiting the club fields of New Zealand's South Island, he was inspired to develop a similar sort of low amenities/high thrills kind of ski/snowboard area. A narrow valley outside of town with a cirque dropping into a series of gullies fit the bill. Brill and his then girlfriend (now wife), Jenny Ader, began buying up land and raising money. With a bit of land secured, they felled a few hundred trees with chainsaws and erected towers for a used chairlift (acquired from Mammoth Mountain) and began the arduous process of securing recreational access to adjacent Bureau of Land Management land. With the addition of a Quonset hut (for the lodge), a modest bar that Aaron built, and a few buses and an old panel van to shuttle skiers around, Silverton was ready to open.

OPPOSITE:
Don't look for
the intermedi-
ate slopes at
Silverton—there
aren't any!

There are some ski and snowboard experiences that are billed as expert oriented—the Chugach (page 17), Chamonix (page 109), and Jackson Hole (page 221) come to mind. Silverton Mountain has taken the notion of "experts only" quite literally; here, there is only advanced and expert terrain, with no cut trails or groomed runs. And Silverton only sells a limited amount of lift tickets (on an average day, about eighty). Most of the season, you have to ski with a guide. Except for the Christmas holiday, it's only open Thursday through Sunday. To get the full experience, you'll probably end up hiking another two thousand vertical feet to an elevation of more than thirteen thousand feet.

It's been described as "lift-accessed backcountry adventure skiing."

Put another way: At Silverton you don't have to participate in a stampede to find deep powder before the hill is all tracked out. And you don't have to step into a snowcat or helicopter (though if you'd like to, the latter can be arranged).

The secondhand lift will not speed you up the hill. You will not run thirty laps in the course of the day. You will not eat a heaping bowl of hot chili by a fireplace that you could park a Hummer in. But you will have access to a wonderful variety of bowls, cliffs, and chutes over 1,800 acres of double diamond terrain in a place where the snowfall averages more than four hundred inches a year. If you hike to Storm Peak, you can enjoy nearly three thousand feet of vertical drop; up there you're at 13,487 feet, which makes Silverton the highest ski area in North America . . . and, many would say, the toughest. (Vertical drop from the top of the chair, incidentally, is 1,900 feet.)

Bag lunches, by the way, are available for $10.

"Coming back to Silverton as a professional snowboarder with the lift in place really opened my eyes to what was available in the San Juans," Cory continued. "I got to visit the first time shortly after they opened to do a photo shoot. We were all blown away by the bare-bones approach Aaron and Jenny had taken. Some people in town were worried that it was going to become a big resort, and they were very relieved to see the end product. As for the mountain, the terrain you're exposed to from one lift is remarkable. After you drop over the first roller, it's very apparent that you're fully exposed. The fact that it's mostly guided skiing speaks to Silverton's extreme nature. Even professional athletes needed someone to show them the ins and outs. Most places, we can show up and do what we want, but not at Silverton. After all, many of the lines end in sheer cliffs. The guides do a great job with the avalanche safety protocol, and they're always searching out fresh powder opportunities." Avalanche safety gear is required for all guests.

"I like the fact that you don't just ride under the chair at Silverton," Cory added. "You do have to hike a bit, and for some people, doing so at thirteen thousand feet is tough. A lot of folks might sit out a lap after a run or two to get their wind back. For me, the hike along the exposed ridgeline is a great experience." On an average day, visitors will get in three to six runs—or ten thousand to twenty thousand exhilarating vertical feet.

In most Colorado ski towns, it's not too hard to find a rustic bar with a mining theme where you might enjoy a cold longneck or other simple libation. Silverton offers such an establishment, fittingly named the Miners Tavern. But many locals have begun frequenting a watering hole you might not expect to find in a mountains town—a rum distillery called Montanya. A host of rum cocktails are served, as well as appetizers. Sip slowly—Montanya's Platino Light Rum earned a gold medal at the San Francisco World Spirits Competition.

CORY SMITH is senior promotions manager at Smith Optics.

If You Go

▶ **Getting There:** The closest commercial airport to Silverton is in Durango, which is served by several carriers, including United Airlines (800-864-8331; www.united.com) and U.S. Airways (800-433-7300; www.usairways.com).

▶ **Season:** Silverton operates from mid-December to early April.

▶ **Lift Tickets:** Full-day tickets, which include a guide for every eight skiers/riders, run $139. Unguided skiing is offered at the beginning and end of the season for $49. Reservations are required (970-387-5706; www.silvertonmountain.com).

▶ **Level of Difficulty:** Advanced/expert terrain only—you need to know what you're doing to ski Silverton.

▶ **Accommodations:** You'll find a host of lodging options at www.silvertonmountain .com/page/town/lodging.

18

DESTINATION

STEAMBOAT

RECOMMENDED BY **Billy Kidd**

"When I was growing up in Vermont in the late 1950s, Buddy Werner was a hero of mine," Billy Kidd recalled. "I had pictures of him on the wall of my room. When I made the U.S. Ski Team in 1962, I was suddenly skiing next to my hero. We raced in the 1964 Olympics together and became good friends. Sadly, Buddy died in an avalanche in St. Moritz later that year. I came to Steamboat the first time in 1964 for his memorial service, and raced here the following year. Over the next few years, I worked hard to make up the fractions of a second that had come between me and a gold medal. At Innsbruck, I'd missed by 0.14 of a second. A few years later, I missed by 0.06 of a second, then by 0.007 of a second! In 1970, I won the gold medal in the World Championships. I had four medals in my pocket, and that opened many doors. I did some television commentary, wrote books, developed and endorsed products. Of all the things I've done, the thing I enjoy most is helping people ski better. I chose to do so in Steamboat, as I couldn't find a better place to live."

Steamboat Springs sits north of the many ski areas along the I-70 corridor, on the western face of the Rockies. The valleys around Steamboat are rife with hot springs; the story goes that the town got its name when early settlers heard the gurgling of the springs and mistook the sound for that of a steamboat chugging down the Yampa River. Upon further investigation, no steamboat was in evidence, but the name stuck. Modern-day visitors to Steamboat will still find no stern-wheelers, but they will encounter some of the world's best powder. "For many, it's powder that defines good skiing," Billy continued. "The Rockies are blessed with it. Being a thousand miles from the ocean and at a ten thousand elevation, our snowflakes are mostly air. At many places, people describe an out-of-this-world powder day as one when you sink to your waist. On those days when we

OPPOSITE:
Steamboat's
annual Cowboy
Downhill.
Rumor has it,
the cowboys like
Bud Light.

get four or five feet of snow, you sink in up to your hat. We call them snorkel days. Some people think I'm joking about the snorkel. There was a famous fighter pilot named Robin Olds who lived in Steamboat. He'd ski the trees and sink way down in the powder. On one of those big powder days, he came out to ski with a snorkel. There was a photo spread of him in one of the ski magazines. We only get a half-dozen days like that a year, but that's why we live here." (Consumers of ski publications may very well have come upon an image of Billy, up to his signature Stetson in powder. "I try to set a good example by wearing a helmet these days," Billy added.)

One fun facet of visiting Steamboat is that you can take pride in knowing that you're skiing in the lines of many past and present Olympiads. The town of Steamboat Springs has fostered more Olympic skiers and snowboarders than any place in America . . . though this has more to do with humble Howelsen Hill than Werner Mountain. "The Steamboat Resort is celebrating its fiftieth anniversary in 2013," Billy explained, "but the Steamboat Springs Winter Sports Club is coming up on its hundredth anniversary. The ski club—and Howelsen Hill—are the reasons Steamboat has produced so many great athletes. Carl Howelsen [born as Karl Hovelsen] was a Norwegian émigré who came to the United States in the early 1900s. He was an accomplished ski jumper, and for a time, he toured the country with the Barnum & Bailey Circus, ski jumping inside a tent, sometimes over elephants, and into the arms of the circus strong man! Howelsen wasn't the first skier in America, but he probably exposed more people to skiing than anyone else. In 1913, he arrived in Steamboat and began work on what would become Howelsen Hill. Carl taught the local kids to ski, and they taught their kids, and so on. You can watch the kids training on the ski jumps at night from some of the bars on Yampa Avenue."

Before Steamboat Springs became an Olympic training ground, it was a cow town—at one time, among the biggest cattle-rearing areas in the country. This aspect of Steamboat's heritage is underscored with the Cowboy Downhill. Billy explained the event's genesis. "Larry Mahan, one of rodeo's greats, called me up and introduced himself. He said, 'I want to learn to ski, and I hear you're the guy to teach me.' I invited him up, and I'd never seen someone learn so fast. The next year when the rodeo was in Denver [which hosts one of the biggest indoor events], Larry brought some of his fellow cowboys over. When you get three or four cowboys together, you've got a contest—whether it's to drink the most beer or dance with the prettiest girl. It was no different on the slopes—so the Cowboy Downhill was born.

"Now we get about sixty cowboys up to Steamboat. They learn to ski in the morning, race in the afternoon. It all happens on the beginner slope. For the first event, they come down through some Giant Slalom gates. They have to stop in the last gate and lasso a female ski instructor. Then they head down farther and they have to saddle a horse. After the horse has been kicked by a few cowboys wearing skis, it gets a little harder. In the second event, we line up all sixty cowboys at the top of the beginner slope and say 'Go!' We have to put up three rows of fences to keep the cowboys from sailing into the crowd, as they're not really good at stopping."

With almost 3,700 feet of vertical drop, nearly thirty feet of powder, freeskiing for children, an easy way down from the top of every lift, western exposure for afternoon sunshine, and free daily lessons from an Olympic silver medalist, Steamboat has something for everyone. (Billy's one P.M. lesson is the stuff of Steamboat lore: "I try to show people how to apply Olympic techniques to their skiing," Billy offered. "By the end of the run, you'll be one step closer to making the Olympic team!") If you miss Billy's one o'clock run, you might find him skiing Shadows toward the end of the day. "Shadows is a legendary powder spot for both Olympic skiers and intermediate skiers who want bragging rights. It's not really a trail, but a run where we thin out the trees. If you're going down the center, there's a tree every fifty or sixty feet. If you go farther right, the trees are ten or twelve feet apart. You might be a blue trail skier going down the middle, and have one of the best powder skiers in the world right next to you. At the top it's pines, farther down, aspens. The aspens are reminiscent of the bamboo poles that used to be used on slalom courses. I think of it as nature's slalom course.

"To ski down Shadows in the powder as that delicious late-afternoon light spreads across the slope—it's my favorite place to ski. You're skiing off into the sunset, into the Wild West. That's Steamboat."

BILLY KIDD first gained worldwide attention when he finished eighth in slalom and twelfth in giant slalom at the 1962 FIS World Championships. In 1964, he became the first U.S. skier to medal in alpine skiing, when he finished second in the slalom at Innsbruck. Over the next few years, Billy laid claim to the title of America's greatest ski racer of that era. In 1965, he won eight consecutive races in the United States, and in 1966 he won several European races, dueling head-to-head with the great Jean-Claude Killy. However, a broken leg in 1967, and sprained ankles prior to the 1968 Olympics,

DESTINATION 19

hampered his chances at Grenoble. After the Olympics, Billy competed as an amateur for two more years, during which time, in 1970, he won the first U.S. gold medal at the FIS World Championships. He then turned pro and won the 1970 World Professional Championships in giant slalom and combined. Billy has continued with his success in the ski industry. He has been ski director at Steamboat Springs, Colorado, for many years, has represented various ski industry manufacturers as a spokesman, been a ski commentator for television, written columns for ski magazines, and written two books on skiing. Billy has served on the President's Council for Physical Fitness and Sports and has been a part-time coach to the U.S. Ski Team.

If You Go

DESTINATION 19

▶ **Getting There:** Steamboat is 160 miles northwest of Denver; several airlines serve Steamboat Springs, including American (800-433-7300; www.aa.com) and United (800-864-8331; www.united.com).

▶ **Season:** Late November through mid-April

▶ **Lift Tickets:** A day ticket at Steamboat runs $99; multi-day tickets are available. Remember: Kids under twelve ski free if a parent purchases a five-day ticket. See details at www.steamboat.com.

▶ **Level of Difficulty:** Steamboat has great terrain for everyone, designated 14 percent beginner; 42 percent intermediate; and 44 percent advanced.

▶ **Accommodations:** A range of lodging options are available through Steamboat (877-783-2628; www.steamboat.com).

TELLURIDE

RECOMMENDED BY **Paul Zabel**

It didn't take very long for Paul Zabel to fall in love with Telluride.

"It was the winter of 1992, and I was living in Detroit at the time," Paul began, "and had driven out to Colorado for an extended ski-bumming trip. I had skied many of the big mountains, and was at Breckenridge when I had a call from my mom. She mentioned that a family friend was also visiting Colorado, at a place called Telluride. I'd never heard of it, but she encouraged me to give her a call, so I did. Mom's friend said, 'You should come down here, it's just unbelievable.' I asked her where it was from Breckenridge, and she said it was five hours south. I drove down. As I drove east on Highway 145 into the historic section of the town, I told myself, 'If you ever take this view for granted, then you should leave.' I spent two days in town. Then I drove back to Michigan, quit my job, canceled the lease on my apartment, borrowed $1,000 from my folks, and drove back. Right now I'm seven months into my twenty-first year.

"It's difficult to say why after two days in Telluride I made the move. The formula includes a number of factors. First, there's the scenery. Most of the land around Telluride [including the ski area] is national forest property; the undeveloped surroundings always put Telluride near the top of the best-of lists for ski area scenery. Then there's the historic Victorian town, the quality of the ski area, the weather (three hundred days of sunshine a year), the friendly locals . . . and the fact that the nearest stoplight is sixty-five miles away, which was quite a change from navigating the six-lane highways around Detroit. Overall, there's a special vibe that makes Telluride a nirvana for someone who likes the outdoors."

Telluride's transformation from mining town to skiing town came relatively recently compared to other Colorado resorts. The first lift went up in 1972; the last mine closed six years later. The area grew slowly at first; development efforts were hampered by several

bad snow years. But founder Joe Zoline persevered. Music and film festivals drew outsiders to the region, and as the area grew, it developed a "best kept secret" reputation . . . which of course drew even more visitors. The mountains around Telluride were rumored to be a drop-off point for Mexican drug smugglers, and this burnished the town with a bit of a Wild West image; it was even featured in the song "Smugglers Blues," by the Eagles' Glenn Frey, on the ubiquitous cocaine-centric TV series *Miami Vice*:

> They move it through Miami, sell it in L.A.,
> They hide it up in Telluride,
> I mean it's here to stay.

As more and more celebrities descended on the southwestern Colorado town, the counterculture reputation gave way to one of rugged mountain chic. But limited development has helped reinforce the proposition of Telluride's tagline: "The most beautiful place you will ever ski."

With more than three hundred inches of dry snow and 3,845 feet of vertical (4,425 feet if you're willing to hike a bit) spread over two thousand acres, Telluride offers plenty of terrain to explore. Paul shared a few of his favorite spots. "Bear Creek is one of those skiing landmarks that is always a point of contention. It's one of the holy grails of off-piste in North America but it comes at a price. The San Juan Mountains have a notoriously unstable snowpack, and Bear Creek has taken many lives. There is also a property dispute with mining claim owners over whether or not skiing there is trespassing. That being said, if you are a savvy backcountry enthusiast and know the lines, it provides for some of the most scenic, steepest, and deepest runs anywhere, runs that extend for over three thousand feet. Chair 9 is an iconic triple on the north side of the area that holds great snow and has long, steep, thinned-out tree shots. You'll enjoy the long, dry, north-facing powder lines and snow-eating grins at the bottom. If you have the energy, another must for advanced skiers is Palmyra Peak. It's more than thirteen thousand feet and an hour's hike from the top of Chair 12. Follow the billy-goat path up and drop into one of the biggest inbounds lines anywhere. The Gold Hill Chutes are to the skier's right—ten more huge hike-to lines that are also inbounds.

"When you get a powder day at Telluride, you'll want to have your skis in line at Chair 8 as early as you can. You're probably fifteenth in line if you get there an hour before the

OPPOSITE:
Main Street in Telluride, the kind of vista that makes downhill enthusiasts pick up stakes and move to Colorado.

20

DESTINATION

lifts start up. Next, run over to Baked in Telluride for a coffee and bagel. Standing in line with all of the hard-core locals, you just feel the energy as everyone anticipates getting into the fresh champagne powder. Every local has their own private hidden stash. You'd make a couple of quick laps off Chair 9, then drop into the trails off of Chair 6 until the patrol drops the rope accessing Gold Hill. When I can't stand up anymore I'll go to Gorrano Ranch—a midmountain food service that used to be an old sheepherders' cabin—to drink a bunch of water, then beer. As friends gather—you never ski with anyone on a good day because it will just slow you down and, as the saying goes, 'There's no friends on a powder day'—you make plans to hot tub somewhere before the après-ski parties. I usually go to the Last Dollar Saloon, locally called the Buck, and then finish at the Sheridan Bar, which has been around since the mining days. Sometimes we'll go out for a nice dinner at Hongas, a pan-Asian favorite, or just grab a dog from Eric's Diggity Dog cart on Main Street."

One of Paul's most memorable days on the slopes at Telluride came in the winter of 1995. "It had snowed for five or six days in a row, with a minimum accumulation of twelve inches per day," he recalled. "I got up early for work and had to wear my bibs for the walk across town. When I got there, I saw other employees heading out the door so I grabbed a snowboard and just went to the lift line. The actor Kiefer Sutherland was in line in front of me and my bosses were behind me. I knew my time was short so I took Chair 7 and then cut over to 9. I didn't like the traffic on the runs off 9 from my vantage point on the chair, so I dropped off the back into Apex Glade. On my way, I saw people just starting to cut over to Gold Hill, so I decided to commit and just go for one glory run. As I made my way across the top to a gladed area, I noticed that the snow was as deep and light as I'd ever seen . . . ever! I made my way down through the trees. Looking back at the snow coming off my board, it appeared just like a water-ski spray. My heel cuts would kick the snow up almost like a tunnel or a wave tube and then I'd board out of it. My whole body was touching the snow on every turn, like dragging your elbow waterskiing. I was sure at the time that that run was the pinnacle of my downhill life and it would never get that good again.

"Thus far, it hasn't."

PAUL ZABEL graduated from Haworth College of Business (Western Michigan University) in 1992 with a degree in management and a minor in general business. He moved to Telluride in 1993. Paul has been involved in a number of successful property management and real estate entities in Telluride. Today he is co-owner of Elevation Vacations and Telluride Property Services. Paul is a passionate skier, and also enjoys traveling, snowmobiling, dirt biking, rafting, hiking, camping, and fly-fishing. His favorite spots outside of Telluride are Spain, Costa Rica (where his son was born), and the Bahamas.

If You Go

► **Getting There:** The Montrose-Telluride area is served by Allegiant (www.allegiantair.com), American Airlines (800-433-7300; www.aa.com), and Delta Airlines (800-221-1212; www.delta.com).

► **Season:** Telluride is generally open from late November through early April.

► **Lift Tickets:** A two-day ticket at Telluride begins at $127. Multi-day tickets are available; discounted tickets may be purchased seven days in advance at www.tellurideskiresort.com.

► **Level of Difficulty:** Telluride's 125 trails are classified as 23 percent beginner; 36 percent intermediate; 41 percent advanced.

► **Accommodations:** Visit Telluride (888-605-2578; www.visittelluride.com) lists hotel options around the ski area. Elevation Vacations (888-728-8160; www.elevationvacations.com) offers a host of rental properties.

20

DESTINATION

VAIL

RECOMMENDED BY **Pete Seibert Jr.**

Pete Seibert Jr.'s Vail roots could not run much deeper. His father, after all, was one of the resort's founders. "My dad moved our family here from Denver in the fall of 1962 in preparation for the first ski season at Vail," Pete remembered. "I was seven at the time. There were four families with school-age kids, and we had one classroom that bounced from space to space. They let us out at 1:30 every day, and we put on our skis and were on the mountain the rest of the afternoon. Some of the trail names describe how it was. Over in Sundown Bowl, there were two trails called Seldom and Never. They're almost all the way across the bowl, facing back at Chair 5. When we'd get a foot of snow, people would ski the lines that were easiest to reach, and then slowly traverse the bowl to find fresh tracks. There were so few skiers, it would take days for people to get all the way across the bowl in search of powder. Seldom was rarely skied; Never was at the very end and saw hardly any skiers. Before you got all the way over to Never it would usually snow again and the whole process would begin all over."

Vail is located along the Interstate 70 corridor, roughly one hundred miles west of Denver. Like Aspen to the south, Vail has nearby Camp Hale and the 10th Mountain Division to thank for its inception. Soldiers slated for alpine combat during World War II came to Colorado to train before shipping to northern Italy; many came back after the war to ski and, in some cases, establish ski areas. Among this group was Pete Seibert Sr. Pete Sr. worked at Aspen for a time and then managed the Loveland Basin Ski Area, but longed to develop a new Colorado resort. He found a kindred spirit in a native Coloradan and uranium prospector named Earl Eaton, whom he met ski racing in Aspen. In 1957, the two first climbed Vail Mountain, and knew they had found their spot. Initial investors kicked in $10,000 each in return for a condo near the mountain and a lifetime ski pass.

OPPOSITE:
Vail is one of
North America's
largest resorts,
with terrain
for all levels of
skiers and riders.

21

DESTINATION

By early 1962, $1 million had been raised, and by December, the Bell gondola from Vail Village to Mid-Vail made its first run. Through the 1960s, new trails were cut, new lifts installed, and Vail expanded. One of its great public relations boosts came when then-representative (and soon to be president) Gerald Ford visited Vail, and eventually purchased property; many Americans' first exposure to the resort no doubt came during news segments showing President Ford's Christmas trips to the mountain. Today, Vail encompasses nearly 5,300 acres of terrain between the Front Side, Back Bowls, and Blue Sky Basin, making it one of North America's largest resorts.

"In the early days, one of the raps against Vail was that it wasn't as steep as some of the other big resorts at the time—Sun Valley, Alta, Stowe," Pete continued. "There was an interview that the well-known University of Denver ski coach Wally Schaeffler did with *Sports Illustrated* where he said that Vail was too flat." (Pete Sr. and his partners turned this seeming slight to their advantage, positioning Vail as a family-friendly destination, complete with a picture-perfect village that would be at home in the Alps.) "After I'd traveled a bit and came back, I had the same impression. Yet what it lacks in huge steeps it makes up for in the sheer breadth of the experience. It would take a dedicated skier a week to get around the whole mountain. Traditionally, many ski areas are north-facing, as they need to be to retain snow. At Vail, you have a host of different exposures, especially in the back bowls, and this allows you to find great stuff to ski throughout the day. Another thing that's special about Vail is that it's easy for everyone to ski the same mountain and still connect for lunch." New skiers can take runs off Chair 14 while more-advanced skiers can run lips on the Buck Bowls, and all meet at Two Elk Restaurant.

Vail may not have the horrifying couloirs and dizzying chutes that define more extreme areas, but it has its share of signature runs. Pete shared a few favorites. "One trail I really enjoy in the Back Bowls is Genghis Khan. It's a relatively steep, very long shot from the ridgeline down to the bottom of China Bowl. You don't see that sort of sustained pitch at a lot of other places that are steeper. It's on the lee side of the mountain; if there's powder around, it gets a bigger deposit of snow. I also like Ricky's Ridge, or Seldom. On the Front Side, I will frequently ski Ouzo, or Ouzo Glade. My favorite last run of the day is Riva Ridge, which is probably Vail's best-known trail. It starts at 11,250 feet and drops 3,050 vertical feet, all the way to the village. The first section is expert terrain, but then it's mostly intermediate. There's one steep section in the middle called Tourist Trap that might be intimidating for some, but you can take a catwalk around it called Compromise.

"As much as I enjoy the powder days at Vail, my favorite time to ski is in the spring when we get corn snow," Pete shared. "It's not as hectic out there as a good powder day can be. I'll head to the Sun Up and Sun Down bowls. There's no end to the lines that you can seek out, and if you play with your exposures, you will probably still find good snow later in the day. People will keep coming back around on Chair 5—it's only a six-minute ride up. You'll see an amazing group of people out there in the spring. Locals will be there first, but eventually visitors will figure it out. Spring skiing at Vail takes me back to the camaraderie that my father and the other guys had in the early days, the shared love of the sport. You could be a billionaire from New York or a college student from CU who's saved up enough to come up for a day. They're both together on the chair, and the differences fall away."

PETE SEIBERT JR. has been a Vail local since 1962, when his father brought the family to the valley to start the ski area. Pete's childhood revolved around the mountain: winters were spent ski racing, summers playing in the woods and streams. Upon graduating from Middlebury College, Pete worked as a Vail ski patrolman, then followed his dad to Snowbasin, Utah. Five years in Utah led to Sun Valley, Idaho, working on Bald Mountain. Pete returned to Vail twenty-six years ago, in time for the birth of the first of four children. After a stint managing the fledgling Arrowhead ski area, Pete went to work at Slifer Smith & Frampton Real Estate, which has kept him busy the last twenty years. Pete spends his free moments skiing, cycling, and enjoying the mountains with his kids.

If You Go

▶ **Getting There:** Guests can fly into Vail on several major airlines, including American (800-433-7300; www.aa.com) and United (800-864-8331; www.united.com).

▶ **Season:** Vail is generally open from mid-November through mid-April.

▶ **Lift Tickets:** Day passes for Vail and nearby Beaver Creek are $80; multi-day tickets are available.

▶ **Level of Difficulty:** Vail's 193 trails are classified as 18 percent beginner; 29 percent intermediate; 53 percent expert/advanced.

▶ **Accommodations:** The many lodging options available around Vail are highlighted at www.vail.com; 800-805-2457.

CHAMONIX VALLEY

RECOMMENDED BY **Aurélien Ducroz**

"Chamonix—and skiing—have always been in my life," began champion freerider Aurélien Ducroz. "Four or five generations of my family have been mountain guides, including my father and grandfather. My mother is a ski teacher. I was born in Chamonix, and grew up in the ski culture. Though it's long been my home and I may be biased, I think there are a number of things that make Chamonix a special place. For one thing, it's a real town, where people are living year-round. It doesn't close down in the summer. Another thing is that there are so many different people living here, both from different countries and living different lifestyles. When you walk down the main street in town, you'll meet people who have come down from Mont Blanc in their mountaineering gear. You'll see people in biking clothing, but you'll also see bankers in suits. The combination, the blend of sport and city life, makes it an interesting, cosmopolitan place.

"Something else I really appreciate about Chamonix is the sense you have of being in a wild mountain place. For a time, I was doing a lot of ski jumping. I was very small and light, the perfect size for jumping; most of the competitions were on concrete hills in the middle of towns. I missed the mountains. At one point, I decided that I could walk away from ski jumping, come home, and do some great freeriding."

Chamonix is situated in the southeast of France. From almost any viewpoint in the valley, Mont Blanc looms tall; at 15,782 feet, it's the highest point in the Alps, touching Italy and Switzerland. The vistas are postcard beautiful. As the pinnacle of western Europe, Mont Blanc has long attracted the adventurous, be they paragliders, ice climbers, or extreme skiers. For this reason, Chamonix has gained notoriety as the so-called "death-sport capital of the world." Before being a death-sport capital, Chamonix was widely considered the world's winter sports capital. Though the first ascent of Mont Blanc was

OPPOSITE:
Skiers at
Auguille du
Midi prepare
to descend
Chamonix's
famed Vallée
Blanche.

made in 1786 and word began to spread, the region began attracting visitors in earnest after 1860, when a road was built from Geneva, in anticipation of a visit from Emperor Napoleon III. The emperor and empress were enchanted with the valley, and ordered that the road be improved. In the winter of 1906, competitive skiing under the auspices of Club Alpin Français appeared in the valley. Less than twenty years later, Chamonix hosted the first-ever Winter Olympics, held in 1924. That first Olympics featured 258 athletes from sixteen nations, participating in eighteen events. (In 2010, some 2,600 athletes from eighty-two nations participated in eighty-six events.)

Thanks to its significant elevation—most runs are above 6,500 feet, and many above the tree line—Chamonix consistently serves up deep snow, and there are more than one hundred miles of trails spread over eight different resorts to enjoy it: Les Grands Montets, Brévent-Flégère, Le Domaine de Balme, Les Houches, La Vormaine, Les Chosalets, Le Savoy, and Les Planards. (The latter four are geared toward novices.) Intermediate skiers/riders will find a good deal of terrain here, though it seems that the lion's share of the runs—and the off-piste environs—were made with the skilled alpinist in mind. Les Grands Montets has mostly advanced terrain, including two exhilarating runs, Pylones and Point de Vue. The latter sails along sections of the Argentière Glacier, offering glimpses into glacial crevasses. If you want to build your wind up before tackling Point de Vue, consider a climb to the observation platform at the top of the Grands Montets cable car. It's 121 steps up, but the views are stunning.

If there's one trail that defines the Chamonix/Mont Blanc experience, it's Vallée Blanche (White Valley), a thirty-plus-mile, 9,209-vertical-foot leviathan. This epic descent along the Mer de Glace (Sea of Ice) glacier begins with a ride on the Aiguille du Midi cable car, which spirits the intrepid from the center of the village of Chamonix to a height of 12,605 feet. There are several ways to make your way down through the vast powder fields, though most newcomers will opt for the *voie normale* (standard route); a mountain guide is advised. En route, you'll pass through huge seracs and past towers of ice and spectacular crevasses. If there's enough snow in the lower reaches, you can ski all the way back to Chamonix. "I love to bring people up to Valle Blanche to see the view and experience the quiet—just the mountains surrounding you," Aurélien said. "When I ski there, I like to take my time. For me, it's about having a good time with friends."

Aurélien vividly remembers the day that the slopes of Chamonix called him home. "I was still competing as a ski jumper, and I was back home skiing with my father. We had fifty centimeters of fresh powder, and no one was around. The skiing was wonderful. We stopped for lunch at one of the refuges on the mountain. As a ski jumper, you have to watch your weight, and I was constantly on a diet. I had begun to think that I had had enough of ski jumping. At lunch that day, I decided to order dessert. A little later that afternoon, my trainer called to remind me that I was supposed to be at a training session at a different mountain that night. I paused for a moment, thinking of the day I'd had at Chamonix with my father, and then replied, 'No. I'm staying home.' "

AURÉLIEN DUCROZ was born in Chamonix and began skiing at age two. When he was fifteen, he joined France's Ski Jumping team and won two titles as Champion de France, and participated in his first World Cups. In search of new challenges, Aurélien returned to Chamonix to hone his freeriding skills. He found great success, being named the Freeride Skiing World Champion in 2009 and 2011. Aurélien was Vice World Champion in 2005, and placed third in 2004, 2007, 2008, and 2012. He's also earned four World Cup victories. In the summer months, Aurélien is a professional sailor. After only three years of sailing, he took part in the most extreme solo transatlantic race: the Transat 650. In July 2012, Aurélien competed in his first race in Class 40.

If You Go

▶ **Getting There:** International visitors will generally fly into Geneva, which is roughly fifty miles from Chamonix/Mont Blanc.

▶ **Season:** Skiing can begin as early as the first week in December and continue as late as the first week in June, depending on which part of the area you're visiting.

▶ **Lift Tickets:** The Mont Blanc Unlimited ticket, which offers skiing throughout the valley (and also in Courmayeur, Italy, and Verbier, Switzerland) is 54 euros. Multi-day tickets, and other lift options, are highlighted at www.chamonix.com.

▶ **Level of Difficulty:** While there is terrain for beginners and intermediates, Chamonix will be best enjoyed by advanced skiers and boarders.

▶ **Accommodations:** The Chamonix Office of Tourism (+33 4 50 53 00 24; www.chamonix.com) highlights lodging options throughout the valley.

DESTINATION 22

VAL D'ISÈRE

RECOMMENDED BY **Jane Jacquemod**

Mention Val d'Isère in a room of well-traveled skiers and boarders, and you're likely to arouse strong emotions. Its proponents may call it a nirvana for skilled alpinists with abundant snow and an après-ski scene that's second to none; its naysayers may call it overrated and overpriced, a mega-resort overrun by British yahoos. Most will eventually agree that it's a place you need to see for yourself.

"Before anything else, Val d'Isère is a high-mountain village, and this makes the area different from many others," Jane Jacquemod described. "It's been a village since at least the eleventh century. At most places, you might have a village down in the valley, and a ski resort above. We have both a village life and a ski resort life. When I first visited as a student in the early 1970s, I thought it was the most fantastic place I had ever seen. I came back again a few months later, and I've been here ever since."

Val d'Isère rests in the Tarentaise Valley of southeastern France, adjoining the border with Italy and Vanoise National Park. (As the crow flies, it's fifty miles due south of Chamonix.) No valley contains more world-class ski areas than the Tarentaise; neighbors include Courchevel, Meribel, Les Arcs, and La Plagne. Early visitors came in the summer to let their animals feed in the high-mountain pastures. By the latter part of the nineteenth century, tourists seeking fresh mountain air were drawn to Val d'Isère for its spectacular scenery. The early twentieth century saw growing interest in winter sports, fueled in part by the success of Louis Bonnevie, a local man who became the French ski champion in 1906. Yet it wasn't until the 1930s that the first lift was installed at Val d'Isère; a full-fledged resort emerged after World War II.

Today, Val d'Isère is divided into three main sectors: Bellevarde (which is home to Val d'Isère's two renowned downhill courses, the OK and the Face); Solaise (which is mostly

OPPOSITE:
At Val d'Isère,
many of the
more challenging
runs are on the
lower half of
the mountain.

given over to easier terrain and boasts ample sunshine during clear weather); and Le Fornet (which has the highest lift service and is home to Glacier de Pissaillas). Val d'Isère is part of L'Espace Killy, which is touted as the highest extended ski terrain in the world; Tignes is the sister resort. L'Espace Killy extends more than ten miles from the Pissaillas Glacier to Tignes's Grande Motte glacier; it's possible to ski or board from one end of the valley to the other. In total, L'Espace Killy boasts over 180 miles of on-piste terrain spread over 158 trails.

"You can easily spend a week's holiday without skiing the same slope twice," Jane continued. "Personally, I enjoy staying up high, above the tree line. These days, I'm not looking for especially tough skiing. I like nice, calm sunny slopes. At Val d'Isère, many of the easier slopes are on the upper half of the mountain. You have to choose a little more carefully to find a gentle way back down into the village. Because we're at such a high elevation [nearly all of the village and mountain is above six thousand feet], we're above the fog that you get in some places. If guests are seeking a trail to conquer, I'll recommend The Face. As the name implies, it's right on the face of Mount Bellevarde, and has everything—steeps and, often, many moguls. It was the site of all the men's alpine events in the 1992 Olympics, and was used for the World Championships in 2009."

L'Espace Killy's vast on-piste terrain is impressive, yet it's dwarfed by the almost endless off-piste opportunities between Val d'Isère and Tignes. For expert skiers/boarders, this is the main attraction. A few of the better-known off-piste tours include Vallée Perdue, Le Tour du Charvet, Le Col Pers, Col du Montet, Col de Vache, and Le Pisteur's Couloir.

If you're not in the backcountry, thoughts will eventually turn to a break and some sustenance. "I should say that most French skiers like their lunch," Jane added. "Certainly, there are youngsters who head out with some snacks in a backpack and ski hard until the lifts close, but most like a nice stop in the middle of the day. Val d'Isère has many excellent altitude restaurants. One that I enjoy is Folie Douce-La Fruitière, which is at the La Daille midstation." La Fruitière has the décor of a milk cooperative, and boasts a cheese cellar. One of its signature dishes is Feuilleté Savoyard, melted local cheese and ham ensconced in a light fluffy pastry crust. "On Le Fornet, there's another place that's quite good, L'Edelweiss," Jane said. "It has a classical menu for the region, and a lovely view from a beautiful terrace.

"When you come off the mountain at Val d'Isère, there's plenty to do. If it's a sunny day, you might stop at the bottom of the slopes at Le Barrillon for a beer or a Coke. It's just a little snack bar, but they have chairs outside. If you go into the village, there are many options. I like Salon des Fous. It's small and lively, a nice place for a glass of wine. There are mostly French speakers here. The Moris Pub is a bit more of a gathering place for British people, and they have live music. I should mention that almost everyone at Val d'Isère speaks English. I know that some people get a bit stressed if they think they have to speak French, but that's not the case here. Language barriers aren't an issue."

If you have energy for a special meal once après-ski activities have concluded, consider a trip to L'Atelier d'Edmond. "The restaurant is built in a chalet," Jane said. "It's a reproduction of a carpenter's workshop, based on the workshop of the founder's grandfather. It's Michelin-starred—you're always going to get something special there."

JANE JACQUEMOD came to nearby Grenoble University in the early 1970s from Bristol, England, and she never really left. Today, she serves as director of press and communications for the Val d'Isère Tourist Board. Though she prefers mellower slopes today, there's adventurous skiing in her DNA; her daughter, Ingrid Jacquemod, has competed in several Winter Olympics (2002 and 2006).

If You Go

▶ **Getting There:** Most international travelers will fly into Geneva (one hundred miles from Val d'Isère), which is served by most major carriers. Regular buses will spirit you to the resort.

▶ **Season:** Val d'Isère is generally open from December to early May.

▶ **Lift Tickets:** Day passes begin at 45 euros; multi-day passes are available.

▶ **Level of Difficulty:** L'Espace Killy boasts 180 miles of trails, classified as follows: 61 percent beginner; 28 percent intermediate; 11 percent expert. Note: Many regulars feel that some of the beginner and intermediate terrain here would be classified as intermediate or expert terrain at other resorts.

▶ **Accommodations:** The Val d'Isère website (www.valdisere.com) lists a range of lodging options.

DESTINATION 23

SUN VALLEY

RECOMMENDED BY **Reggie Crist**

If Sun Valley were to launch a new ad campaign, the slogan might be "Come for the history, stay for the skiing."

At least that's how two-time Skier X winner Reggie Crist might write it.

"You have to start with the history of the place," he began. "Sun Valley was America's first destination ski resort. It was home to the first ski lift in North America, and was the epicenter of downhill skiing for many years. When you visit the Sun Valley Lodge and see all the old photos, you get a feeling for the history of the place. That history adds to the allure. From a skiing perspective, many have the perception that Sun Valley is a fairly easy mountain. It's true that it's always had lots of big runs that are groomed to a fault. But with the better, lighter equipment that's come along in the last few decades, more people are venturing off-piste, and there's a lot to explore on Baldy [Bald Mountain]. It gives you a lot of vertical in a short amount of time. The lifts go straight up the fall line and the runs come straight down. There's a sustained, consistent pitch. When you ski Sun Valley, you're going to get tired, as you're always making turns. Local skiers are very strong thanks to all those turns—that's why you get so many good racers coming out of here."

Sun Valley owes its existence in large part to the vision of Averell Harriman and the Union Pacific Railroad. Harriman, who had developed a passion for skiing while traveling through Austria and Switzerland, wanted to develop a winter resort in the West—at least in part to drive traffic to his railroad. In 1935, he retained Count Felix Schaffgotsch, scion of an Austrian banking family who Harriman had met in his European travels, to scout out potential sites. After nearly a year of searching, Schaffgotsch came upon the old mining town of Ketchum in the Wood River Valley of central Idaho. Upon arrival, he wired Harriman: "This combines more delightful features than any place I have ever seen

OPPOSITE:
The slopes at
Sun Valley
rise right from
town, and are
known for their
sustained pitch.

24
DESTINATION

in Switzerland, Austria, or the U.S. for a winter resort." Acreage was soon purchased, and by the winter of 1936, Sun Valley had opened its doors. Harriman and his team had a flair for public relations, and they quickly put the new resort on the map by inviting Hollywood royalty—the likes of Clark Gable, Errol Flynn, and Bing Crosby—to be guests of the lodge. They came, they skied, and the place that was marketed as "the American Shangri-La" was on the map.

Geopolitical conditions at the time of Sun Valley's inception conspired to quickly make Sun Valley the epicenter of American skiing. "With Germany invading Austria and the general unrest in Europe in the late thirties, many of the ski instructors were fleeing Europe," Reggie explained. "Harriman was sparing no expense in building Sun Valley into a world-class resort—as good or better than anything in Europe—and he hired the Europeans as instructors. You had many of the world's best skiers in Sun Valley mixing with Hollywood's elite, who were coming in on the overnight train from Los Angeles. It must have been interesting to see those colliding cultures."

Many celebrities still come. A partial list of the rich and famous who regularly pass through the Sun Valley region includes Mark Zuckerberg, Oprah Winfrey, Bruce Willis, Tom Hanks, and Arnold Schwarzenegger.

The chance to rub shoulders with glitterati may be enough of an allure for some, but most come for the hill. Most agree that Count Schaffgotsch did well. Bald Mountain ("Baldy" among regulars) is the core of Sun Valley, with 2,054 acres of inbounds terrain and 3,400 vertical feet accessed through sixty-six trails. (The other hill at Sun Valley, Dollar Mountain, has historically been geared toward beginners, though its freestyle amenities—including a twenty-two-foot super pipe and seventy-six rails spread over four parks—are making it "Park Central" for boarders and free skiers.) Harriman's branding concept proved more than wishful thinking; Baldy and its surroundings are bathed in sunshine much of the ski season, which doesn't hurt the resort's appeal. How does an X Games champion ski Sun Valley? Reggie shared some of his strategies.

"I don't necessarily have a favorite run at Baldy," he opined, "but I'll head for where I can find the best conditions . . . and this is often off the map. One on-the-map run that's tough to beat, though, is a top-to-bottom high-speed run down Warm Springs—3,100 vertical feet of sustained pitch that is wide open and perfectly groomed. This run is guaranteed to make your eyes water and your legs burn. If I'm trying to find powder, I head for The Bowls [along the top of Baldy]. This is wide-open powder skiing for hard-charging skiers who like to let it run. This is my training grounds and the best place to strengthen my legs for big-mountain skiing in places like Alaska. As I mentioned earlier, Sun Valley doesn't get recognition for its out-of-bounds skiing. You can drop off the mountain 360 degrees around and end up at your car. If conditions are right, I like the Castle Rock Burn. In 2007, a fire took down almost fifty thousand acres of forest on the north-facing slopes of Baldy. Now it's a naked forest you can ski through."

Where might you find Reggie at the end of the day, if he happens to be skiing Baldy? There's a decent chance he'll be at Apples Bar and Grill. "It's at the base of the Warm Springs Lift," Reggie added, "and it's one of Sun Valley's iconic watering holes. After a day of long runs, beer and a burger never tasted so good."

REGGIE CRIST's career goal is to ski as much powder as humanly possible. He was a member of the U.S. Ski Team for ten years and is one of the most accomplished X Games athletes of all time, having won the Skier X competition twice. When not on the race course, Reggie and his brother Zach are staple big-mountain skiers with production companies such as Warren Miller and Rage Films. They have also been featured in several adventure films, claiming first descents on the polar ice cap of Greenland, the Himalayas of Nepal, the Alps of New Zealand, and the coastal giants of Alaska. In the summer months, look for Reggie in the whitewater, riding big waves or kayaking Class 5 rapids.

If You Go

▶ **Getting There:** Sun Valley is served by Alaska Airlines (800-252-7522; www.alaskaair.com) and SkyWest (800-221-1212; www.delta.com).

▶ **Season:** Sun Valley is open Thanksgiving through mid-April.

▶ **Lift Tickets:** Day tickets during the regular season at Sun Valley are $95; multi-day tickets are available.

▶ **Level of Difficulty:** Sun Valley offers terrain for skiers of all ability levels. Its eighty runs are classified as 36 percent easy; 42 percent more difficult; 22 percent most difficult.

▶ **Accommodations:** Sun Valley Resort (800-786-8259; www.sunvalley.com) offers a wide range of lodging options.

DESTINATION 24

KASHMIR

RECOMMENDED BY **Chris Patterson**

As principal director/cinematographer at Warren Miller films for two decades, Chris Patterson has scouted out some of the world's most out-of-the-way skiing venues. "Once I earned my wings at Warren Miller and had filmed at many of the more conventional mountains, I began pursuing places that captivated me," Chris explained. "I keep a folder of exotic places—Ecuador, Morocco, India. Adventure is part of my DNA; I'm the kind of person who, when I see an article in *National Geographic* about Mongolia that's talking about the nomadic life of herders, my eyes are drawn to the mountain that's way in the background of the accompanying photograph. I'm wondering, *Can we film there?*

"One of the out-of-the-ordinary trips that sticks out for me is Kashmir, in northern India. I've actually filmed there twice. Both the skiing and the overall experience are phenomenal. You have the allure of the big, big mountains—we were often skiing at elevations between twelve thousand and fifteen thousand feet, with mountains like Nanga Parbat exceeding twenty-five thousand feet in the distance. Our helicopter pilot was on oxygen! The quality of the snow is amazing, and there are massive quantities of it. Plus, there's the edginess of being in a conflict zone, as Gulmarg, where we were based, is right near the border with Pakistan; it's just twenty-five miles away from the place where Osama bin Laden was found and killed. We didn't see any conflict, just lots of soldiers milling around, though apparently there is the odd stray rocket that gets lobbed over the mountains from time to time. As I was up in the helicopter a fair amount of time, I couldn't help but hope that there wasn't a soldier at a rocket station nearby who dozed off, woke up suddenly to the sound of a helicopter, and instinctively pressed the fire button. Gulmarg has a scattering of hotels. Some are labeled five-star, though the five-star hotel I stayed at didn't have heat or hot water."

For some, Kashmir may more frequently reside in the file folder of dangerous conflict zones rather than a dream ski destination. Situated in the northwestern region of the Indian subcontinent—between India, Pakistan, and China—Kashmir has been contested by all three countries for generations, though particularly between India and Pakistan. It's no wonder the region has been an object of desire; thanks to its incredible natural beauty, the area—particularly the Kashmir Valley—has been called a paradise on earth. Gulmarg, the valley's main resort area, sits in the Pir Panjals, one of the six ranges that comprise the Himalayas. It's been called "the heartland of Indian winter sports"; though one must admit that India is not generally recognized for its abundance of winter sports.

While heli-skiers will find themselves quite alone on the mountains around Gulmarg, those visiting the resort in town will encounter nothing like solitude. "There's a beginner slope with a rope tow," Chris continued, "and there, many people are visiting from India's southern cities, wearing their normal day-to-day attire. I'd say that it's the same atmosphere that you see on Indian roads, except the people are on skis. If someone like me were to drive in India, I'd have an accident within ten seconds, but somehow the local people make it flow. People are going the wrong way on the hill, young people are pushing their mom or uncle up the slope on skis. Men who have built wooden sleds will offer to tow you up the hill for a few coins. There's no order at the lift line. People cut in front of each other randomly. At the larger ski area, there are two gondolas, one that takes you to midstation, another that takes you to the top. At the time, instead of paying a daily lift ticket, you paid for each stage of the ride, four or five dollars. Very few people ski the top half of the mountain, which is well above the tree line. It's big-mountain powder skiing; there are some signs and boundaries, but you can pretty much go wherever you want. [The top lift drops you off at nearly thirteen thousand feet.]

"On my last trip, we had some weather and couldn't go up in the helicopters, so we tried to take the tram up. When we got to the gondola, there was a sign:

UPPER GONDOLA CLOSED, NO MORE BOMBS.

It turns out that the resort gets its explosives for avalanche control from the military. That day, the army had said that they couldn't spare any munitions for skiing."

Gulmarg's wide-open terrain (and attitude) allows for some interesting touring potential. "You could start skiing down from the top of the gondola, and then skin over to a spot where you could ski down into a different valley," Chris said, "where there were no skiers at all. We skied all the way down to a town called Tangmarg. The town is on the bus line that heads over the mountain pass into Pakistan. It's a crossroads of sorts, and there's a hubbub of activity. People negotiating fees, travelers with chickens, all their belongings wrapped up in rugs. We had two female skiers with us, with blond hair and Day-Glo clothing. We stuck out like Martians. The bus was very full inside, and we opted to sit on the roof. It was snowing hard, and the bus had bald tires and had overall seen much better days. We figured we'd have a better chance of survival from the top of the bus; if it started to go off the road, we could jump off. Though Kashmir is a conflict zone and the culture is very unfamiliar, it never felt like a truly dangerous place. I think you could find more trouble driving through certain parts of Los Angeles."

Chris's defining Kashmiri moment came during a day of filming. "We didn't have the greatest weather forecast that day," he recalled, "but the skies that morning were clear, and we had a short window to shoot. When you're on a film assignment, you have a hit list of the kind of footage you need to get. In this case, I wanted to get some shots of a skier with the big mountains in the distance while the weather was clear, some close-ups, which we could get even if the weather went south, and some shots that captured the grandeur of the mountains. Our helicopter pilot was a New Zealander—very talented, but also a bit on the reckless side. (Most of the Kiwi pilots are cowboys.) Generally, when I'm shooting from a helicopter, I strap myself in the doorway. I thought it would be interesting to try to get the shots from the basket instead of from the doorway, and I asked the pilot if he'd be willing to try that. He was. I asked if it was safe, and he replied, 'Nothing is safe, we're at fifteen thousand feet in the mountains.' I did it anyway.

"We sped out through these gnarly mountains, racing toward the leading edge of the Karakorum Range, and I'm sitting out in the basket. There was no better view of these mountains on the planet, nothing could compete. I kept asking myself, Is this really happening? I got my scenics, and then we returned to our skiers, who were positioned at the line of control. The backs of their skis were in Pakistan, the tips in India.

"I've filmed many great vistas over the years. But seeing them waiting there for our signal, at this altitude, was a view and an experience that trumped them all."

CHRIS PATTERSON has spent the last nineteen years as the principal director/cinematographer of the annual Warren Miller Films and spends five months each year shooting their latest action sports feature film. He recently worked as director of photography of an action unit on Christopher Nolan's feature film *Inception*, and has also worked as cinema-

DESTINATION

25

tographer on films and TV spots for directors Klaus Obermeyer (Visa, Lipitor, Navy), Jake Scott (HP), Tony Scott (Army), Baker Smith (Air Force), Rob Cohen (Dunkin' Donuts), Leslie Libman (Extreme Team), and Zalman King (Wind on Water). He is the cofounder and cinematographer for Confluence Films, which creates fly-fishing movies that bring his action filming aesthetic to the world's best fly-fishing waters. Chris has shot hundreds of projects for international resorts, manufacturers, branded entertainment, television programs, and documentary films in forty-plus countries and on some of the highest mountains around the world. In the last ten years, he has helped create many automobile advertisements, working with Ford, Nissan, Buick, Toyota, Hyundai, Jeep, and Lincoln. Chris also finds time to have fun; he's an expert skier, snowboarder, climber, and kayaker, and loves mountain biking, hockey, and fly-fishing. When he's not on assignment, Chris is at home with his family in Montana.

If You Go

▶ **Getting There:** Gulmarg is a two-hour drive from Srinagar, the capital of Kashmir. Srinagar is served by several airlines (via Delhi and Mumbai), including Air India (800-223-7776; www.airindia.com).

▶ **Season:** Mid-December through mid-April; the heli-ski season is a bit shorter.

▶ **Lift Tickets:** The ride to mid-mountain is 150 rupees; to the second stage, 250 rupees. An unlimited gondola day pass costs 1,250 rupees (about $24). Kashmir Heliski (www .kashmirheliski.in) offers daily and weeklong heli-skiing adventures out of Gulmarg; a six-day all-inclusive skiing package is listed at 450,00 rupees. Maqsood Madarie (www .newjacqulinehouseboats.com) can help you coordinate the logistics of your trip.

▶ **Level of Difficulty:** There are no trail maps or trail ratings for Gulmarg. The heights alone—often above twelve thousand feet—would suggest that only very fit individuals travel to Gulmarg to ski.

▶ **Accommodations:** As Chris described, the hotels in Gulmarg will not likely exceed your expectations. A few that have received more positive reviews include The Vintage (www.thevintage.in/gulmarg.htm), Khyber Resorts (www.khyberhotels.com), and the Heritage Hotel Highlands Park (www.hotelhighlandspark.com).

CORTINA D'AMPEZZO

RECOMMENDED BY **John Frasca**

"There is something very special about the Dolomites," John Frasca opined. "The shapes of the rocks and their colors are something you have to see. When the sun shines on the mountains, you feel as if you're skiing amongst gems—sometimes pink, sometimes orange. It's an amazing experience, especially as the sun begins to set."

When people (at least *Italian* people) think of skiing the Dolomites, they think of Cortina d'Ampezzo.

Cortina rests in the Veneto region of northeastern Italy in the enchanting Ampezzo Valley. The resort sits at an elevation of four thousand feet in the southern Dolomites, a section of the Southern Limestone Alps. The mountains' jagged shapes and glowing coloration largely exist courtesy of their main component, dolomite, a kind of carbonate rock. Roughly two hours north of Venice, Cortina may be the world's most popular ski resort for non-skiers. Since the resort was established, Italy's glammerati have flocked there to see and be seen, frequently enshrouded in fur. (Some have estimated that up to 70 percent of Italian wintertime visitors to Cortina do not ski.) "Cortina has long been known as a jet-set destination," John continued, "though it's a place where the famous can go and maintain a level of privacy. If Europeans want to show off, they go to St. Moritz. That being said, Cortina is a fashion show of sorts. One person is better looking than the next. The scenery is spectacular on the mountain and on the Corso Italia, a pedestrian zone known for its restaurants and boutiques."

But for a moment, back to the slopes.

Though skiers have schussed around the valley of Cortina since the turn of the last century (and tourists have come for almost another century), the region did not gain international exposure until 1956, when the VII Winter Olympic Games were held here.

OPPOSITE:
This couloir highlights the colorful dolomite that makes up the mountains around Cortina D'Ampezzo.

DESTINATION

26

125

(The games were initially slated to be held in Cortina in 1944, but the war intervened.) Financial shortfalls in preparation for the games prompted organizers to seek corporate sponsorship, setting a precedent that would become as much a foundation of the Olympics as the Giant Slalom. Today, the fifty-plus lifts around the town's center serve some ninety miles of on-piste terrain; if you're adventurous enough to rent a car, you can access eight other resorts and over seven hundred miles of terrain throughout the Dolomites for roughly the cost of a week's ticket at one resort, through the Dolomiti Super Ski Pass.

"Cortina came to the attention of Americans after the '56 Olympics, though I think it may be better known to a younger generation as the location of some of the scenes from the Sylvester Stallone film *Cliffhanger* and the James Bond film *For Your Eyes Only*," John continued. (In the latter case, it was the site of the famous stunt scene where assassins riding spike-wheeled motorcycles pursued 007 across the slopes.) "As affluent as the clientele at Cortina are, I find it a down-to-earth environment. And since so many of the Italian visitors don't ski very much, American guests will find the slopes uncrowded—and frequently sunny. Four out of five days have clear skies." (Some joke—or at least half-joke—that the average Italian ski day begins at eleven A.M., and consists of one run to a mountainside restaurant where a large lunch washed down with a few glasses of wine is consumed. Lunch is followed by a nap in the sun and then a short run down to one of the grappa bars in the village.)

The terrain at Cortina is spread among four areas around the Ampezzo Valley. These include Faloria-Cristallo-Mietres, Tofana-Socrepes, Cinque Torri, and Lagazuoi. (You cannot ski from one area to the other, though they are connected by lifts or shuttle buses.) Each is distinct. You'll find the region's steepest trail at Cristallo in the shape of Forcella Staunies, which launches skiers/riders with a slope of 65 percent and continues through a narrow gorge bookended by cliffs. The exhilaration of the pitch is only enhanced by spectacular views across the Dolomites and down to the center of Cortina. Tofana is the highest point at Cortina, reaching 10,640 feet. "On a clear day, you can see Venice Bay," John added. Beginners and intermediates will find numerous runs here; advanced skiers will want to head to the Socrepes area, where more challenging terrain awaits. Cinque Torri, while a bit smaller than its counterparts, tends to have the lightest crowds.

Lagazuoi is at the end of the valley, and is home to one of Cortina's signature trails—the Hidden Valley run. A cable car takes you along a cliff face, where observant eyes will spy windows—entries to a series of tunnels leading to observation posts and gun stations from World War I. (At the time of the war, Cortina was part of the Austro-Hungarian Empire; the village was abandoned by the Austrians when Italy joined the conflict in 1915, but battles ensued in the mountains through 1918.) The trail itself rolls five miles through a quiet valley far removed from the hubbub of Cortina proper, past towering cliffs and sparkling frozen waterfalls, en route to the village of Armentarola. Near the midway point, you may opt to stop for lunch at Rifugio Scottoni. (The mountains around Cortina are dotted with fifty such chalet-style shelters—*rifugi*—where meals and simple lodging are available. Meals here almost universally exceed the overcooked and overpriced fare found at many resorts.) You'll need to hop a bus to get back to town at the run's conclusion.

For something a bit different, visitors have the option to combine downhill skiing with a little history on the Great War Ski Tour, which takes you on an eighty-kilometer journey (via bus, lift, and slopes) through the old battle zone. The tour includes the Hidden Valley Run.

JOHN FRASCA is the president of World on Skis (www.worldonskis.com), a full-service ski vacation planner offering domestic and international ski vacation packages, as well as customized ski packages that encompass all the elements of your dream ski vacation.

If You Go

► **Getting There:** Most visitors to Cortina will fly into Venice, which is served by many international carriers. It's a two-hour drive from Venice to Cortina.

► **Season:** Cortina is open from late November through mid-April.

► **Lift Tickets:** Day tickets begin at 38 euros; multi-day tickets are available. Details are available at www.cortina.dolomiti.org. Many making the trek to Cortina will purchase the Dolomiti Superski Pass (www.dolomitisuperski.com), which gives you access to twelve areas in the region. Cortina is geared toward more-casual skiers/riders. Terrain is rated as 50 percent beginner; 35 percent intermediate; 15 percent advanced.

► **Accommodations:** The Cortina tourism website (www.cortina.dolomiti.org) lists a variety of lodging options in this popular Italian resort area.

NISEKO AND BEYOND

RECOMMENDED BY **Tommy Moe**

"A lot of people call Japan 'Japow,'" Olympic gold medalist Tommy Moe offered. "I did a cool trip over there a few years ago to do a photo shoot with Spyder Clothing. We flew into Tokyo, and then on to Sapporo on the island of Hokkaido. From there, we drove to Niseko. Between my skiing at the resorts at Niseko and nearby at Asahidake, I'd have to say that 'Japow' is pretty accurate!"

Niseko is in the southwest of Hokkaido, Japan's second-largest island. It's only a few miles inland from the island's west coast; on rare clear days, the Sea of Japan is in view, and ever-so-faintly, the Russian coastline. Like the word "Aspen," Niseko can mean different things to different people. For some, it references the town; for others, it speaks to Niseko Annupuri, the most eastern peak of the Niseko Volcanic Group. (It's contained in the Niseko-Shakotan-Otaru Kaigan Quasi-National Park.) For the skiing/snowboarding community, the term means the region's five ski resorts and a seemingly endless supply of powder. Four resorts at Niseko—Niseko Annupuri, Niseko Village, Grand Hirafu, and Hanazono—are interconnected (and co-marketed) under the rubric Niseko United; you can ski/board all four areas—a total of almost 2,200 acres and sixty-one runs—under one pass. Niseko Moiwa is a smaller resort on the western side of the mountain.

Skiing/boarding at Niseko is not about reaching vertiginous heights. Niseko Annupuri tops out at less than 4,300 feet, though its vertical approaches a considerable three thousand feet. Here—and throughout Hokkaido, for that matter—it's about the snow. Winds that sweep across Siberia pick up moisture from the Sea of Japan, and that moisture is deposited as delicate powder on Niseko and other Hokkaido hillsides. (At Niseko, snowfall averages nearly six hundred inches a year.) Those Siberian winds are cold, and cold temperatures mean absurdly light powder. "We skied at Niseko for three days," Tommy

OPPOSITE:
Fresh tracks
at Niseko,
with Mt. Yōtei
providing
a dramatic
backdrop.

DESTINATION

27

continued, "and if you got off the groomed runs, there was powder, sometimes bottomless powder. I had the sense that Japanese skiers don't go off-piste very much. During my visit, they opened up the backcountry. The way the snow piled up there was unbelievable."

The four areas at Niseko are not known for their incredible steeps. Instead, more advanced powderhounds head for the trees. At Hanazano, it's the tight trees in Blueberry Fields and the more widely spaced trees in Strawberry Fields; at Hirafu, the Miharashi Trees. If the backcountry behind Hanazono is open, even more glades (and bowls and gullies) await, and when conditions permit, huge powder fields are a twenty-minute hike from the top lift. "Skiing through the trees was an exotic experience," Tommy recalled, "as the snow really clung to the birch trees. At one point we were going through these open forests and the snow hung on the branches in all of these different formations. They resembled snakes. Off in the distance you could see volcanoes, including Mount Yōtei, which looks a lot like Mount Fuji. At the end of the day, we dropped into the onsen [hot springs] at our hotel. The water was close to 110 degrees. You get a little sweat going as you soak your bones."

Onsen are widespread around Niseko, thanks to the volcanic activity in the region. Braving the waters is an essential part of the Japanese ski experience—whether you espouse the health benefits many associate with the mineral waters or not. There are a few points of onsen etiquette you might want to take note of:

• Baths are generally single sex; blue curtains indicate the men's bath, red the ladies'.

• Bathers are expected to bathe naked (it's believed that nakedness breaks down societal barriers and enhances the overall sharing experience of the baths).

• Bathers should take off their shoes before entering the changing room, and leave their clothes in a basket provided.

• Bathers can wear a small modesty towel between the changing room and the wash room.

• Bathers should wash thoroughly before entering the bath.

From Niseko, Tommy and the photography crew headed northeast to Asahidake, a mountain in the Ishikari Range near the center of the island. It's Hokkaido's tallest mountain, with an elevation of 7,616 feet. Asahidake's elevation helps create snow that makes powderhounds who are already giddy with Hokkaido's possibilities almost punch-drunk. Here's how the website Powderhounds describes the experience:

Asahidake has an abundance of powder with an average of about 14 metres of snow per season, but no one really bothers to put too much emphasis on measuring the amount of snow because there's so much of the white stuff. Asahidake is pretty much the crème de la crème of the powder that Hokkaido skiing is renowned for. This is the highest mountain in Hokkaido so the snow is kept super cold. And unlike Niseko, Asahidake is not near the ocean, so the powder isn't just dry; it's often sublime!

"Asahidake is really more like a sightseeing area serviced by a cable car than a ski area," Tommy said, "though the cable cars take skiers/boarders up in the winter. The day I was there, there were only four other people riding up. The snow was waist-deep—sometimes even chest-deep—and we had the whole place to ourselves. We sessioned a lot of the terrain under the tram, and had all fresh tracks. Then we hiked up from the top of the tram, as the photographers were hoping to get shots of some deep-powder turns. We went about twenty minutes, and then set up for the shot. I began down, but I couldn't make any turns. It was so deep, all I could do was go straight. It was a truly amazing experience."

TOMMY MOE knew that skiing would be part of his future since his grade school days when his father let him play hooky to ski powder. What he didn't know was that he would become a World Cup contender and take home the gold in the 1994 Olympics in Lillehammer, Norway, where he won the downhill by .04 of a second, followed by a silver in the Super-G. Today, Tommy is a partner and founder of Tordrillo Mountain Lodge. He finds the greatest reward in sharing the property and newly discovered terrain with skiers and snowboarders seeking the trip of a lifetime, whether it's a week of powder skiing in the winter, whitewater rafting the Tal and Coal Creek, or paddle boarding under the summer midnight sun. Tommy has been skiing and rafting the Alaska wilderness for over twenty-five years; he has intimate knowledge of the mountains and rivers, and is a certified WFR since 2000. He resides in Jackson Hole, Wyoming, with his wife, Megan Gerety, and their two young daughters, Taylor and Taryn.

DESTINATION

27

If You Go

▶ **Getting There:** Visitors to Niseko fly into Sapporo, which is served by many carriers, including All Nippon Airways (800-235-9262; www.ana.co.jp) and American Airlines (800-433-7300; www.aa.com).

▶ **Season:** Niseko is generally open early December through early May.

▶ **Lift Tickets:** Day tickets at Niseko (www.niseko.ne.jp) are 5,900 yen, during the high season; multi-day passes are available. Day tickets at Asahidake (www.wakasaresort.com) cost 4,000 yen.

▶ **Level of Difficulty:** Niseko's terrain is classified as 30 percent beginner; 40 percent intermediate; 30 percent advanced. Ideally, you'll have some powder experience. Terrain at Asahidake is almost all off-piste, and better suited toward more advanced skiers/riders.

▶ **Accommodations:** Niseko has a number of lodging options. Some information is available at www.niseko.ne.jp, though the Powderhounds (www.powderhounds.com) website is a bit easier to interpret. Lodging is more limited at Asahidake; Powderhounds also highlights options here.

DESTINATION

27

RUSUTSU

RECOMMENDED BY **Greg Doyle**

"I have skied extensively in Japan, from Tokyo on up to the northern island of Hokkaido, over thirty resorts in all," Greg Doyle began. "There are some seven hundred ski areas total, so I still have lots of exploring to do. But when it comes to powder skiing—especially in the trees—Rusutsu is the best I've experienced. It's not overly steep. People who haven't skied a ton can pick it up and be skiing a straight line with powder blowing over your shoulders after a few days. More experienced skiers and snowboarders will get a thrill from the snow. It seems to fall constantly. There's an average of fifteen meters a year, and it's incredibly dry powder—less than 5 percent moisture. I've skied Utah and the powder is fabulous, but the snow on Hokkaido is dryer and lighter."

Hokkaido is one of the world's larger islands, and makes up over 20 percent of Japan's total landmass. Sturdy but relatively low mountains run through the center of the island, making it the home of a dozen prominent ski areas. Hokkaido came to the world's attention as a ski venue in 1972, when the Winter Olympics were held in the island's main city, Sapporo. (The slalom and giant slalom events were held at Mount Teine; the downhill was held at Mount Eniwa.) Today, the ski town of Niseko and its four resorts (Annupuri, Niseko Village, Grand Hirafu, and Hanazono) on the southwestern end of the island attract many visitors, though nearby Rusutsu has a following among powderhounds. The terrain at Rusutsu is rather modest in proportions: Its peak elevation is not quite 3,300 feet, and its vertical drop is less than 1,800 feet. But the quality and immense amounts of Rusutsu's powder may make you forget about its somewhat diminutive dimensions. "Many Aussies go to Niseko," Greg continued. "It may have the best terrain on the island, but it's so popular. You have to get on the lift by eight A.M., to get freshies, as the powder is pretty much trashed by 9. Conversely, at Rusutsu, there's fresh powder everywhere you look. If you go for a week, you're guaranteed to have two or three days of deep powder. Storms coming through are almost constant. I've been heli- and cat-skiing in remote places where I haven't experienced snow like this. I can feel confident sending people there, as they are sure to get powder."

Rusutsu encompasses three peaks (West Mountain, East Mountain, and Mount Isola) and approximately 420 acres of on-piste trails, though powderhounds like Greg waste little time with the resort's trails. Off-piste skiing is permitted, and Greg likes to focus his energies in the trees at Mount Isola. "A great thing about Rusutsu is that you don't have to spend much time hiking or scouting around to get to the interesting off-piste terrain," Greg explained. "There's a minimum of traversing. You come off the lift and it's pretty much fall line skiing.Rusutsu has a great lift infrastructure, with a total of nineteen, and four gondolas. The lifts have hooded chairs, which makes the ride up nice and cozy." (It's not uncommon to find temperatures hovering around 10°F.)

One note: You won't find steep pitches or great drop-offs on Rusutsu's best powder runs. If such thrill-seeking is up your alley, you might choose a different hill . . . or exult in the joys of making your way through dry powder. Though celebrated for its powder, there's a good deal of fine-groomed terrain at Rusutsu as well, perfect for the intermediate skier to dabble in powder (as there are usually nice stashes at the edges of the groomed trail).

Rusutsu doesn't see many western visitors, and most skiers/boarders stay overnight at the resort. "Though you're only a half hour or so from Niseko, only a small busload of day-trippers come each day," Greg said. "The hotels are amusingly kitsch. There are fountains, singing bears, a waterslide, even a Ferris wheel. You can be sitting in the wave pool and watch people skiing out in the 20-below [centigrade] weather. All of the staff at the hotels are friendly, very friendly. You're almost pulling your hair out after a few weeks, as they're so nice. There's no attitude whatsoever. They provide service. There's a bit of a language barrier if you don't speak Japanese, but in the bigger Rusutsu hotels you can generally find someone who can speak English. Near the resort, there's a street with fabulous authentic Japanese restaurants. When you walk past, they don't even look as though they're open, yet, when you step in the door, you're in a little room with twenty people. They serve authentic ramens, and prices are very cheap."

One day at Rusutsu particularly stands out for Greg Doyle, capturing the deep-powder experience that Hokkaido serves up so consistently. "My partner [and co-owner of Powderhounds.com], Lyndell, and I met a guy from Switzerland who was staying in the same lodge where we were staying. He had a nice, bright yellow jacket that I thought would look good in photos, so I asked him to join us. We got to the mountain early and we were kicked off the last lift. It was a frigid cold day, but we couldn't stop. There was fresh powder everywhere—not ankle-deep stuff, but waist deep. I have visions of skiers coming down where I can only see the tip of their helmets. I have photos of Lyndell deep in the 'white room,' where you can only see her right arm and head.

"It was the most exhilarating powder skiing we've ever had, the excitement of true weightlessness."

GREG DOYLE is founder and co-owner of Powderhounds.com, a group of ski and snowboard enthusiasts who have traveled the world in search of the best powder stash. Based in Australia, he's been skiing for more than twenty years, from the American West to Hokkaido and the Alps.

If You Go

▶ **Getting There:** Visitors to Rusutsu generally fly into Hokkaido at the New Chitose International Airport in Sapporo, which is served by many carriers, including All Nippon Airways (800-235-9262; www.ana.co.jp) and British Airways (800-433-7300; www.aa.com).

▶ **Season:** Rusutsu is generally open late November through early April.

▶ **Lift Tickets:** Day tickets at Rusutsu (en.rusutsu.co.jp) are 5,100 yen; multi-day passes are available.

▶ **Level of Difficulty:** Rusutsu has a great variety of terrain for skiers/boarders of all levels. It's a great place for those with little deep powder experience to get indoctrinated.

▶ **Accommodations:** Rusutsu Resort and Rusutsu Resort Tower (+81-136-46-3111; en.rusutsu.co.jp) are at the base of the mountain. Some choose to stay in the ski town of Niseko, roughly 30 minutes away.

GREATER BOZEMAN

RECOMMENDED BY **Pat Holland**

Bozeman is well known as a hub for trout anglers eager to explore southwest Montana's many blue-ribbon streams, and as a gateway to Yellowstone National Park. It should be better known as a skiing destination, where visitors can mix top-notch regional skiing with the experience of a first-rate destination resort.

OPPOSITE: Lone Peak, gateway to Big Sky's more extreme terrain.

"Bridger Bowl's mission is to provide affordable skiing to the citizens of the local community, namely Gallatin County," Pat Holland began. "The price is right—lift tickets are $49, and a season's pass is $550. There's a foundation that raises money to buy day passes for kids and school children that can't afford it. Lift lines are a rarity except on big powder days, and everyone is extraordinarily friendly. Visit Bridger a few times and you feel like you know everyone at the mountain. It's a social experience as well as a downhill experience. Despite the large contingent of college-age and accomplished skiers, Bridger is very family-friendly, as attested to by its outstanding ski school. Big Sky, on the other hand, is a destination resort. It's big-mountain skiing with wonderful terrain. There's a little more glitter and glitz at Big Sky than at Bridger, a greater emphasis on après-ski."

Bridger Bowl is located sixteen miles north of Bozeman, home of the Montana State University Bobcats. Bridger's existence is testament to the perseverance of die-hard local skiers who saw the possibilities a mountain posed and worked to make it materialize, not for profit, but for love. After a false start in 1951, as Bridger Mountain State Park (with the state of Montana's support), local enthusiasts re-trenched, forming the Bozeman State Park and Recreation Association, open to membership for Montana residents age eighteen and older. In 1955, the original platter lift delivered its first skiers to the mountain. As demand has increased over the years, so have the facilities—it now has a total of eight lifts. "I have to say that we're very proud of what we've built," Pat

137

continued. "The community put it together. We have no debt. When we have the resources, we make improvements."

Though it's a "local" ski area, Bridger is renowned for its challenging terrain—particularly an area called The Ridge. The Ridge sits at the top of Bridger Mountain, at an elevation of 8,800 feet. Before the addition of the Schlasman's Lift in 2008, reaching The Ridge required a hike of some five hundred vertical feet; the new lift cut four hundred feet off the trek. While the hike has been made a bit easier, getting down remains one of Montana's—indeed the West's—great challenges. It's steep, the chutes are narrow, there are lots of trees and lots of rocks. Bridger's regulations state that The Ridge contains "numerous steep chutes, which may end in unmarked cliffs," and strongly recommends skiing with a partner . . . preferably someone who knows where they are going! (Skiers/boarders are required to wear avalanche transceivers.) "If you want to ski some nasty stuff, The Ridge has it," Pat said. "One of my favorite lines is called The Nose. Because of the hiking involved, these spots don't get tracked out, and there's often lots of powder. We have a number of fun events at Bridger. One is King and Queen of the Ridge, where contestants compete to see how many Ridge hikes/runs they can squeeze in over five hours."

Sixty miles south of Bozeman, a somewhat different mountain experience awaits. Where Bridger seems to take a quiet pride in its up-by-the-bootstraps approach, Big Sky dares to think big; in fact, the resort, which was conceived by the late NBC news anchor Chet Huntley and opened in 1973, has trademarked the slogan "The Biggest Skiing in Amerca." Big Sky has the stats to back up this bold claim: 5,532 acres of terrain (together with neighboring area Moonlight Basin); 220 runs totaling 110 miles; and 4,350 feet of vertical. "For Bozeman residents, Bridger can be a morning or afternoon venue," Pat continued. "Big Sky is an all-day event. There's an incredible diversity of terrain. If you like bumps, try Broken Arrow and Mad Wolf on Andecite Mountain. For the best snow, ski off the Challenger Chair on Lone Mountain. Big Sky also offers some long, wide cruisers that are well suited for beginner and intermediate skiers. People that only ski occasionally can feel comfortable here."

The infrequent skier/boarder will do well to steer clear of the trails off Lone Peak, gateway to Big Sky's extreme terrain. The Lone Peak Tram spirits the intrepid to the summit of Lone Mountain (11,166 feet). The climb, 1,450 vertical feet over a distance of 2,828 feet, was considered vertiginous enough that the interiors of the gondolas were originally painted pink to calm passengers. "There's some challenging skiing up on Lone Peak," Pat added. "You really need to know what you're doing. Lenin and Marx—two runs that come down the face—are about the most difficult terrain you can get into without going off into chutes. If you get a clear day, the views of the Gallatin Range to the south and east [in Yellowstone National Park] can be outstanding. Some days, you can see all the way down to the Grand Tetons."

PATRICK HOLLAND began skiing forty-seven years ago at age fifteen at Timberline on Mount Hood, Oregon, when a day pass was $6. Since arriving in Montana in 1986, Pat has skied about thirty-five days each season and, for the past five years, an additional ten days a year in the backcountry. Both of Pat's children grew up skiing at Bridger Bowl, and both were part of the Bridger Bowl Freestyle Team. "We skied as a family both days of the weekend at Bridger Bowl or on the road competing. We skied most areas in Montana, Wyoming, Idaho, Utah, Washington, Oregon, the Tahoe area, and a few in Colorado." Pat has served for six years on the Bridger Bowl Board of Directors.

If You Go

▶ **Getting There:** Bozeman is served by a number of carriers, including Alaska (800-252-7522; www.alaskaair.com), Delta (800-221-1212; www.delta.com), and United (800-864-8331; www.united.com).

▶ **Season:** Bridger is generally open early December through early April. Big Sky opens around Thanksgiving and closes mid-April.

▶ **Lift Tickets:** Adult day tickets at Bridger Bowl (www.bridgerbowl.com) are $49. Adult day tickets at Big Sky (www.bigskyresort.com) are $89, with multi-day tickets available.

▶ **Level of Difficulty:** Bridger rates its seventy-one trails as 20 percent beginner; 30 percent intermediate; 20 percent advanced; 30 percent extreme. Big Sky rates its 155 runs as 14 percent beginner; 26 percent intermediate; 40 percent advanced; 20 percent expert.

▶ **Accommodations:** Bridger offers many stay/ski packages in and around Bozeman; call 800-223-9609 for more details. Big Sky is a full-service resort; learn more about lodging options at www.bigskyresort.com, or call 800-548-4486.

CANNON MOUNTAIN

RECOMMENDED BY **Rich Smith**

When asked what's special about Cannon Mountain, Rich Smith was succinct: "It's all about the skiing and boarding. There are no condos, the base lodge is old. There aren't many amenities. But it's such a strong, challenging mountain. Cannon is an out-west-style hill, with gnarlier conditions. There are days when we're skiing on solid ice—but that's okay, as people who ski here are skilled and come to be challenged. But it's not icy all the time. We also have days when there's thigh-deep powder.

"There's an intangible quality about Cannon that gives regulars a strong bond. I was out on the mountain last fall doing some dry-land work. One member of the work party was a new coach at Franconia Ski Club, who'd come from a different mountain. As we were working, he said, 'I don't know what it is about Cannon, but I wanted to come back here so my kid could have this experience.' Many of the guys who skied here when they were young want to come back and coach and be part of the community."

Cannon Mountain is 190 miles north of Boston in the town of Franconia, at the north-western edge of New Hampshire's White Mountains. Anyone who has driven through the Granite State has seen Cannon, though they may not realize it. A rock formation that once adorned part of Cannon—the Old Man of the Mountain—graces road signs, license plates, and New Hampshire's statehood quarter. (The formation collapsed in 2003, though the road signs live on.) Cannon's existence as a ski area owes much to the construction of North America's first passenger tramway. The tramway was the brainchild of Alexander Bright, a member of the U.S. Olympic Team who'd witnessed such trams in Europe in 1933. Bright helped garner legislative support over the next few years, and Franconia and Cannon Mountain was eventually selected as the site. Though a few trails already existed on the mountain by the time the tramway was completed in 1938—including the Richard

OPPOSITE: Cannon's Taft Slalom Trail, originally cut in 1933 . . . before there were any lifts.

DESTINATION

30

141

Taft Race Course—the tram showed the viability of skiing as a tourist attraction. Cannon also benefited from the establishment of the Franconia Ski Club in 1933, and the 1939 arrival of Baron Hubert von Pantz from Kitzbühel, Austria, who developed the Mittersill ski area on adjoining Mount Jackson.

"The tone for Cannon is set by the vista you get looking across from the lift," Rich continued. "You look out at Mount Lafayette, which is over five thousand feet tall. Some people look at the Franconia Ski Club website and ask, 'Why do you have a western mountain on your home page?' It's not, it's Lafayette. For challenging on-piste terrain, many look to the trails that we call the Cannon Front Five: Avalanche, Paulie's Folly, Zoomer, Rocket, and Gary's. Of these, Avalanche is the longest, and has the most pitch—forty-eight or fifty degrees. Avalanche, incidentally, was the site of the first World Cup event in America, in 1967. The rest of the mountain has twisting, old-school New England–style trails. It's fun terrain to ski. And Cannon produces a lot of great skiers, including Caitlin Ciccone and Julia Ford."

For northeastern skiers of a certain generation, the Mittersill holds a forbidden-fruit fascination. Once a companion area to Cannon, Mittersill fell on hard times in the early 1980s and by 1984, was "officially" closed . . . though members of the Cannon community surreptitiously cleared lines and poached the area, despite state and federal restrictions. For some, Mittersill is the New England equivalent of the beyond-the-gates terrain at resorts out west like Jackson Hole—an un-groomed, un-policed adventure area of double fall lines and birch glades, with the ghostly presence of old lift towers poking above the undergrowth. And like Jackson Hole, the 1,850 vertical feet at Mittersill are again open to the public, and even serviced by a lift. "Cannon is working to keep Mittersill as natural as possible, leaving the glades intact," Rich said. "It's all natural snow. You can make it over to the top of Mittersill from Cannon on the Taft Race Trail. It's like going to a fantasy land—no ropes, no anything, just skiing great terrain."

Alpinists outside of New England may not know much about Cannon, but they've probably heard something about its most renowned local son, one Samuel Bode Miller. "Bode grew up nearby, and would free-ski on Cannon all the time," Rich recalled. "He would rip the hill. I think the challenges of skiing here helped make him such an incredible skier. I remember when he first started using the K2 4's up at Carrabassett Valley—and winning events by huge margins. In 1996, he made the U.S. Team, and won three Junior Olympic titles. I was up at one of the events in Maine, as I was then coaching the ski team at the Holderness School. A storm blew in as we were driving home. It took forever to get back. I finally reached my house, and the phone rang. It was a friend. 'You've gotta ski tomorrow,' he said. 'It snowed two feet, and it's the last day of the season.' I told him that I was whooped, but he wouldn't take no for an answer. The next morning, I pulled into the parking lot, and who pulls in next to me but Bode. He'd just finished up six days of aggressive, competitive skiing, but there he was. There were about fourteen of us there that day, and we skied as a group, right until closing. I think that says a lot about Bode's love for skiing, and a lot about the devotion people have to Cannon.

"Many people may not remember it, but in 1967, Jean-Claude Killy won a World Cup event at Cannon, sweeping the downhill, the giant slalom, and the slalom, all in one weekend. The next skier to sweep all three events in one weekend was Bode Miller. One won at Cannon. One grew up at Cannon."

Coincidence? Perhaps not.

RICH SMITH grew up skiing in Massachusetts, and farther north through the Old Colony Ski Club. He spent a few years at Waterville Valley and Breckenridge, before starting to coach ski racers at Holderness School in New Hampshire in 1986. After a dozen years at Holderness, he coached at Cannon Mountain through Franconia Ski Club. He left Franconia for several years to work at the United States Ski Association, and returned to take on his current role as program director at Franconia Ski Club.

If You Go

▶ **Getting There:** Franconia is roughly a hundred miles from Burlington, Vermont, and 190 miles from Boston. Both are served by a number of carriers.

▶ **Season:** Cannon is typically open from late November through early to mid-April.

▶ **Lift Tickets:** A day pass at Cannon runs $70.

▶ **Level of Difficulty:** Cannon's seventy-three trails and glades are classified as 21 percent beginner; 47 percent intermediate; 32 percent expert.

▶ **Accommodations:** Cannon Mountain (603-823-8800; www.cannonmt.com) lists a number of lodging partners and stay and ski packages.

DESTINATION

30

TUCKERMAN RAVINE

RECOMMENDED BY **Jake Risch**

The words "extreme skiing" and "New England" are not frequently uttered in the same sentence . . . unless the topic happens to be Tuckerman Ravine. For eastern alpinists, "Tuck" is the very definition of skiing on the edge. Many western skiers and riders will be surprised to find such daunting terrain so close to Boston that you can pick up Red Sox games on your old-fashioned non-satellite radio!

"Growing up, my father, Al Risch, guided trips on Mount Washington," Jake Risch began. "My first time skiing Tuckerman was on one of his trips. Growing up in the valley, I'd always been aware of the mountain. It's a rite of passage on everyone's radar, the only above-tree-line alpine terrain on the East Coast. It's the place in New England where you can get that backcountry big-mountain experience. The first time I skied the headwall, I was eight or nine. It was a great education; that experience has taken me from the Alps to heli-skiing in Alaska. It all started at Tuckerman."

Mount Washington is the tallest peak among New Hampshire's White Mountains; at 6,288 feet, it's the highest mountain in New England. The mountain is infamous as the site for the highest wind speeds ever recorded (231 miles per hour, recorded at the summit on April 10, 1934), and bitter spring weather that can change on a dime. Oddly enough, given its atmospheric vicissitudes, the summit can be reached via automobile on the Mount Washington Auto Road, dubbed "America's Oldest Manmade Tourist Attraction"; the first tourists traveled to the top via horse-drawn wagons in 1861. Where drivers to the summit will likely acquire a THIS CAR CLIMBED MOUNT WASHINGTON bumper sticker, those ascending the southeastern side of the mountain earn the élan of conquering—or at least attempting to conquer—what's been called the original home of American extreme skiing.

OPPOSITE:
Skiers eye their lines from the bottom of the bowl at Tuckerman Ravine.

DESTINATION

31

145

Tuckerman Ravine is a glacial cirque that gathers great amounts of snow from surrounding alpine faces, thanks to those aforementioned winds. The cirque was first explored on skis in 1914, though it would be another seventeen years or so before skiers broached Tuckerman's upper reaches. Members of the Dartmouth College Outing Club pioneered many ski routes on Mount Washington, and it was two Dartmouth skiers—John Carleton and Charley Proctor—who were the first to ski the Tuckerman Headwall, on April 11, 1931. As skiing gained in popularity, local chambers of commerce began promoting the cirque. It was the American Inferno, a summit-to-base race run, held several times in the 1930s, that attracted the most attention to Mount Washington and Tuckerman.

Skiers and boarders approach Tuckerman much the same way today as competitors in the first Inferno did in 1933. Jake Risch describes the routine: "There have never been any lifts at Tuckerman, so you're either hiking up or skinning up. The season typically begins at the end of March, goes as long as the snow lasts. People do ski all season, but you need extensive knowledge of skiing in avalanche terrain and solid beacon/shovel experience to attempt it in the winter. In the spring, I'll try to get to the trailhead at Pinkham Notch early, say six or seven A.M.; the earlier you get up to the summit, the better the skiing. Before you even leave for the trailhead, you need to check the weather forecasts and the Mount Washington Avalanche Center so you understand what you're getting into. After all, it's one of the deadliest mountains in the United States, with 139 fatalities to date. Understanding the hazards—getting as much info as you can, and making sound decisions—is an important aspect of skiing Mount Washington.

"If there's enough snow in the lower reaches, you can ski up to the top using alpine touring equipment on the Sherburne Ski Trail. If it's later in the season, you'll probably end up hiking at least part of the way, and might opt for the Tuckerman Ravine Trail. About 2.5 miles up, most people will stop for a little break at Hojos [a caretaker's cabin] and check in with the snow rangers or volunteer ski patrol. At this point, you'll probably determine if you're going to ski Hillman's Highway [a 1,400-foot vertical drop, considered one of the easier routes down] or the bowl proper. Assuming you're opting for the bowl, you'll continue up, and soon you'll reach it—a massive amphitheater. Most people will set up a camp for the day on the floor of the bowl, pick a line, and spend the rest of the day skiing as much as they can. People who are in good physical shape may be able to get in two or three runs in an afternoon."

There are a number of named lines in Tuckerman proper. These include Left Gulley, The Chute, Center Gulley North and South, The Icefall, The Lip, The Sluice, and Right Gully. "I don't really have a favorite run," Jake added. "They're all very good; what skis best depends on snow conditions and where the sun happens to be."

As alluded above, caution can be the better part of valor at Tuckerman Ravine. "Back in college, I used to enjoy sharing the ravine with friends who were unfamiliar with the region," Jake recalled. "There was one day when some guys were really excited to go, but the avalanche danger was very high. I had to call everyone and cancel the trip. It was very hard to do, but sometimes it's the only responsible course of action."

JAKE RISCH is an avid backcountry skier, trained heli-ski guide, and lifelong "Tucks" skier. He served as a captain in the U.S. Army and has extensive military and civilian logistics expertise in remote areas, including both Afghanistan and Iraq. A charter life-time member of Friends of Tuckerman Ravine (www.friendsoftuckerman.org), Jake was elected the organization's president in 2012.

If You Go

▶ **Getting There:** The closest commercial airport is in Manchester, which is served by several airlines, including Southwest (www.southwest.com), United (www.united.com), and Delta (www.delta.com).

▶ **Season:** While it's possible to ski Tuckerman in the winter, most visitors ski the cirque from March through June . . . or however long the snow lasts.

▶ **Lift Tickets:** Your legs are your lift at Tuckerman. Be prepared for at least three miles of strenuous hiking before your first (and probably only) run of the day.

▶ **Level of Difficulty:** High. There are fatalities every year at Tuckerman, so take heed. Visit Friends of Tuckerman Ravine (www.friendsoftuckerman.org) and the Mount Washington Avalanche Center (www.mountwashingtonavalanchecenter.org) to learn more about the mountain.

▶ **Accommodations:** Lodging is available at the base of the mountain at Joe Dodge Lodge (603-466-2727; www.outdoors.org/lodging/whitemountains/pinkham). Nearby North Conway (www.northconwaynh.com) offers other lodging options.

TAOS

RECOMMENDED BY **Tait Wardlaw**

Tait Wardlaw has his parents to thank not only for his existence, but for his introduction to Taos at the tender age of seven.

"My parents started skiing Taos in the early 1960s, not long after the mountain opened," he recalled. "They lived in a commuter town outside New York City called Tuxedo Park, and would go to Taos and Alta on vacation. For them it was about adventure, not luxury. When I was five or six, my dad—who was working on Wall Street as an invest-ment banker—said enough's enough. He wanted us to live somewhere we could have a better quality of life. By the time I was seven, we were in Taos. I had learned to ski at Sterling Forest, a small New York ski area with several hundred feet of vertical. Suddenly I was living at the base of the mountains of Taos Ski Valley. Taos is at an unusual cross-roads, in terms of the quality of its terrain, the amount of snowfall, the dryness of the snow, and the amount of sun. After years of skiing in such a place, it would've been easy to have made the assumption that every ski area was big and steep, full of great tree ski-ing, deep powder, and sunshine. Yet, even as a boy, skiing with powder up to your waist, on such steep slopes, with so much sun—I knew it was special."

The town of Taos rests in the middle of the Sangre de Cristo Mountains that stretch from south central Colorado through northern New Mexico, south to below Santa Fe. Taos Ski Valley—eighteen miles north of the town—was born after founder Ernie Blake spied the basin north of Wheeler Peak from the cockpit of his Cessna 170. Blake, who already worked in the ski industry, wanted to launch an operation of his own. By 1955, he'd moved his family to an eleven-foot-long trailer in the valley, and by 1956, a J-bar lift had been installed, leading skiers to Taos's first (and then, only) run—the trail now known as Snakedance. Today, there are 110 trails and 13 lifts, encompassing 1,294 acres of skiable

OPPOSITE:
If the 110 trails at Taos aren't enough, you can hike to fresh snow along West Basin or Highline.

DESTINATION

32

terrain. The resort is still operated by the Blake family, Ernie's grandchildren. "From the beginning, Taos has been a hard-core skier's community," Tait continued. "In many ways, it's modeled on a European-style ski environment. Jean Mayer, who founded the ski school and more than fifty years later still acts as its technical director (and also built and operates Hotel St. Bernard, a popular inn at Taos), came from France. Today, you'll often hear French, German, and Spanish spoken on the mountain."

The stage for Taos is set before you even slide into your boots. "As you arrive in the Ski Valley, you come around a curve, and you're faced with a very steep mountain, dominated by mogul boulevards and several chutes, dropping from the top of your sight line down to the parking lot. There's a massive sign hanging over the ticket booth that reads DON'T PANIC. YOU HAVE ONLY SEEN $1/30$TH OF THE MOUNTAIN. WE HAVE MANY EASIER SLOPES, TOO. This section of the mountain includes two of Taos's jewels: Al's Run [named for Al Rosen, a Taos surgeon who continued to ski the mountain for twenty years after a heart attack, equipped with an oxygen mask and tank] and Snakedance. These two mogul runs are really pitchy and bumped up, but they're soft moguls. If you're at Taos, you've got to ski these runs under Chair One—though pretty much wherever you are on the mountain, you've got steep skiing, top to bottom, without much traversing.

"If you're game for some hiking, you can head up to Highline Ridge or West Basin Ridge, off Chair 6. From here, you can look west into Arizona and north into Colorado. You can do a short hike along West Basin to some world-class chute skiing, and wind up back at the same lift. If you head east along the ridge to Highline, the terrain is a little more open. There are some classic views here; thirteen-thousand-foot Wheeler Peak is right before you. There are some cornices you can ski off from Highline, or you can keep going all the way to Kachina Peak, which is a forty-minute hike. When you finish your run and look up, you feel like you've accomplished something."

One of the pleasures of skiing/boarding Taos is the opportunity to take in both the town of Taos and the community of Taos Ski Valley, which happens to be the highest-elevation municipality in the United States (with a high point of 12,581 feet). "Taos has many compelling characteristics," Tait continued. "You have a mix of three cultures: the Pueblos, who've been here for eight hundred years; the Hispanics, who've been here more than two hundred years; and the more-recently-arrived Anglos. There are many artists here, perhaps more per capita than anywhere else. The quality of the light and the land-scape above the Rio Grande Gorge are unlike anywhere else; the sunsets are ridiculously beautiful. Taos Ski Valley has a different vibe. Some call northern New Mexico the land of mañana—people take their time, put off what they can. The Valley has this extremely laid-back vibe with the skiing focus of a European resort. There's an authenticity here, but it's low key. It feels more like a community than any other resort I've visited."

The attitude at Taos may be best reflected in the martini tree, a phenomenon introduced by founder Ernie Blake. Here's how former *New York Times* music critic Donal Henahan recalled the fabled tree's discovery in the winter of 1958–59:

> He was skiing with a woman who found it impossible to continue down the slope because the light had gone bad. Ernie says he suddenly thought of a "great medical innovation" that might cure the trouble: He sent his 15-year-old son down for a Mexican porron filled with his favorite remedy, the dry martini. It worked miraculously and since that time Taos skiers have come to know that on certain days, if they look diligently, they might find martini-filled bottles hanging from trees along their way. Ernie insists that the spraying of martini into the mouth is not only therapeutic but entirely safe. "It is aerated and very relaxing."

The martini tree, alas, no longer yields its special juniper fruits at Taos. Yet the fact that such a tree once existed certainly speaks to the spirit of the place!

TAIT WARDLAW is vice president of brand marketing/communications for Rossignol Group. Before joining Rossignol, Tait served as vice president/brand director for Dynastar, and marketing director at the Whiteface Lodge.

If You Go

▶ **Getting There:** Many visitors will fly into Albuquerque and drive the 135 miles to Taos. Albuquerque is served by most U.S. carriers. Santa Fe, which is closer, has service from American Eagle (800-433-7300; www.aa.com).

▶ **Season:** Taos Ski Valley operates from mid-November to early April.

▶ **Lift Tickets:** Full-day tickets are $75; multi-day tickets are available.

▶ **Level of Difficulty:** More than half of the mountain is classified as expert terrain.

▶ **Accommodations:** You'll find a host of lodging options at www.skitaos.org/lodging.

CRAIGIEBURN RANGE CLUB FIELDS

RECOMMENDED BY **Nick Castagnoli**

"As my senior year of college was finishing up, some friends and I were encouraged to spend some time skiing down in New Zealand," Nick Castagnoli recalled. "We had friends who were Kiwis that helped point us in the right direction, and everything just fell into place. When I was done at CU Boulder, I threw all my possessions in a friend's garage and took off. On the South Island in Christchurch, our friends told us about the regular car auctions where you can pick up a used car for a reasonable price. We bought a car and ended up renting a house with a cool Canadian couple in the town of Springfield, which is close to the Craigieburn Range. We spent two months there, skiing and exploring the surrounding Club Fields with the 'Chill Pass,' which at the time gave unlimited access to five of the region's Club Fields."

The Club Fields are, as the name implies, patches of mountains managed and run by private ski clubs for the enjoyment of their members—though they are open to all comers for a reasonable fee. If you're looking for high-speed quads, gondolas, or even chairlifts, you'll have to look elsewhere. At the Club Fields—including those in the Craigieburn Range (Broken River, Craigieburn Valley, Mount Cheeseman, Mount Olympus, Porters, and Temple Basin)—guests are, at times, conveyed uphill by unruly tow ropes. Simple huts provide limited food and drink, but enough to sustain the hard-core. "During my stay, we went to the club field where the snow was best at the given time," Nick continued. "Mount Cheeseman was a little pedestrian, and Porters wasn't quite as dynamic. Mount Olympus, Craigieburn, and Broken River became our go-to spots. Overall, they seemed to have more vertical, more challenging terrain."

Of the South Island Club Fields, Craigieburn is probably the best known—some have called it "Steep, Deep, and Cheap!" Terrain is decidedly geared toward experts, with a mix

OPPOSITE:
The Club Fields offer no frills/ many thrills skiing and riding, what many consider to be the quintessential Kiwi ski experience.

DESTINATION

(33)

of large open bowls and short, steep chutes. Kiwis call it "The Big One," thanks to the pitch of its upper reaches and its abundant terrain—almost a thousand acres inbounds, and many more off-piste . . . though even the inbounds terrain has a decidedly unencumbered feeling. "There are not really trails there, and there are only a few patrollers around," Nick said, "so you can pretty much do what you want. It's a massive playground, with very few rules. You have to know your limits. Craigieburn is connected to Broken River by a trail, somewhat the way that Alta and Snowbird are connected. I didn't have skins with me at the time; if you were equipped that way, you could go back and forth pretty easily."

One constant you can expect at whatever Club Field you visit is the nutcracker—a rather primitive tow rope that may prove as daunting to ride up as some of Craigieburn's chutes are to ski down. "Basically, you get up to this tow rope and you try to clasp this hinged metal contraption—the nutcracker—around it," Nick explained. "The tow ropes are going way too fast, especially at Craigieburn, where the ascent is also quite steep; once you connect, you get dragged up the mountain, trying to stay upright and not get your finger caught in one of the pulleys . . . which I did once, fracturing my pinky." Patrollers at the resort and club members will be happy to show newcomers how to negotiate the nutcracker, and there are ample resources online to prep in advance. You'll want to be in good condition before you push off to the Club Fields. Riding the nutcracker takes some upper-body strength.

"Overall, skiing the Club Fields was so much different than anything I've ever experienced," Nick added. "You can't be guaranteed great snow. When a storm comes you've got to be there and ready to pounce. It doesn't get tracked up quickly, but the wind and ever-changing weather can have their way with the conditions in a hurry. But in terms of great terrain and a unique one-of-a-kind experience, you won't be disappointed."

One of Nick's most memorable days skiing the Club Fields was the day he broke his finger at Broken River. "It was a perfect bluebird powder day," he recalled. "The tow rope up to Nervous Knob wasn't spinning so we lapped the ten to twenty minute bootpack, accessing the short chutes and the wide-open bowls, which drop approximately a thousand meters down to the road, if you happen to miss the traverse back around to the resort. We connected with some like-minded travelers from Canada and had the area all to ourselves that day. It was in the afternoon, as I was getting towed back up for another lap, that I zoned out, looking at the surrounding terrain, and allowed the tip of my glove to be pulled into the bullwheel, snapping my left pinkie like a twig. Down at the lodge, the ski patrol tossed me a few ibuprofen and taped my finger up. It was such a good day, I traded out my gloves for a friend's mittens and kept charging. As the sun was setting, we took our final run down as far as the snow line would allow us, then bootpacked across streambeds and back down through the forest to the car. My swollen, twisted finger was throbbing, but it had been an amazing and memorable day, skiing with great friends. Not to mention the Kiwis have free health care."

Nick did offer one disclaimer about the Club Fields experience: the kea, a large parrot that's endemic to the alpine regions of South Island (and the world's only mountain parrot). "The kea are curious and precocious little birds," he added. "They'll eat your windshield wipers, and scoot away with a glove, a hat, or anything else you put down. They're as much a part of the Club Fields skiing experience as the nutcracker."

NICK CASTAGNOLI is manager of public relations/product information at Rossignol. Before joining Rossignol, he attempted a career as a full-time ski bum, but is accident-prone and opted for solid heath insurance instead. Nick's travels have taken him from the untamed slopes of Iowa and the surrounding Midwest, to the Colorado Rockies, and Utah's Northern Wasatch range, where he currently resides.

If You Go

▶ **Getting There:** Visitors fly into Christchurch, which is served by Air New Zealand (800-262-1234; www.airnewzealand.com) among other carriers. Craigieburn's club fields are about a ninety-minute drive northwest.

▶ **Season:** The hills are open June through October.

▶ **Lift Tickets:** Day tickets at most of the Club Fields run $70 (NZ). Five-day passes that allow you to visit any of eleven club fields are $310 (NZ).

▶ **Level of Difficulty:** Craigieburn and Olympus feature mostly expert terrain; Broken River has intermediate as well as expert terrain.

▶ **Accommodations:** Limited dormitory-style lodging is available at Craigieburn Valley (www.craigieburn.co.nz). Cottage-style accommodations are offered at Flock Hill Lodge (www.flockhill.co.nz). Tourism New Zealand (www.newzealand.com) lists lodging options throughout the South Island.

SOUTHERN ALPS

RECOMMENDED BY **Mark Sedon**

Mark Sedon has a friendly warning for anyone who's considering a heli-ski adventure in the Southern Alps: "If you do it, you may be ruined for life. Once you have a taste, it's a powerful drug that you'll want more of. One day is never enough . . . but it's better than none."

The Southern Alps run 270 miles along the west coast of the South Island of New Zealand. Mount Cook is the highest point in the Alps at 12,316 feet, and a number of other peaks eclipse the three-thousand-meter point. Farther south, the mountains are somewhat shorter, topping out near nine thousand feet. They are quite dramatic, however, having been cut through with jagged fjords. (The best known fjord is Milford Sound, the South Island's most renowned attraction and the finishing point of one of the world's most celebrated hiking trails, the Milford Track.) Queenstown is the center for outdoor adventure travelers on the South Island, somewhat akin to Bend in central Oregon or Jackson in the Grand Tetons.

There are several ski resorts in the Queenstown area, yet heli-skiing opens up an amazing variety of terrain—more than 1,100 square miles, in seven different ranges. "I was working at one of the resorts fifteen years ago," Mark recalled, "and I got a chance to go heli-skiing. Suddenly, I was touching down on sides of the mountains I used to have to climb to, or could only gaze up at. Now that I'm a guide, I have the lucky job of flying around to choose the runs that look safe . . . and fun. We fly into the Harris Mountains, the Richardsons, the Remarkables, and the Buchanans—sometimes even north to Mount Cook. Each range has its own characteristics. Closer to the big lakes, the hills are quite steep. If you go farther west, toward the Tasman Sea, there's more glacial terrain. We go where the snow is good. Many times, people are intrigued when we set out. Queenstown

OPPOSITE:
Your pilot has 1,100 square miles and seven mountain ranges to choose from to find you fresh tracks near Queenstown.

DESTINATION

34

157

is only at an elevation of one thousand feet, and there isn't much snow around. People are playing golf in the valley. When you get up to six thousand or seven thousand feet, however, having enough snow is not a problem. It's quite a culture shock."

Mark described a typical day heli-skiing out of the Queenstown area. "The morning starts at eight A.M. We'll drive everyone up to a staging area where the helicopter will pick us up; most are sheep paddocks. After an avalanche and helicopter safety briefing, we load up and the first helicopter takes off. We operate smaller helicopters—European AS355 twin-engine Squirrels and AS350 Squirrels—and have a ratio of four or five clients to each guide. We can land in some small spots! How steep a line we'll choose will depend on the snow. If it's stable, we'll go for the 'movie' lines. If we feel it's uncertain, we'll take lower-angle runs. Though we'll generally have a few groups at a time, you won't see any other skiers on your runs—there's just so much terrain. We'll all connect at lunchtime. We'll make some tables out of snow and have a nice buffet lunch—oftentimes, in the sunshine. After a few more runs, the helicopter will take you back to the valley floor.

"We have more than four hundred runs on two hundred different peaks to choose from, and conditions will dictate where we go on a given day. If the weather is ideal, I love to go west to one of two glaciers—Tyndall or Headling. You start at an elevation of about eight thousand feet, and you get a run of three thousand vertical feet, past crevasses and ice seracs. The snow at the top can be affected by the wind, but as you drop down, you're in boot- to knee-deep powder. Another favorite is up north in the Buchanans, a spot called Galactic Bypass. It's a big, high run near the edge of Aspiring National Park. You're looking out at some of the biggest mountains in the area. On an especially clear day, you can even make out the ocean—it's only twenty or thirty kilometers away. On the way back to town, we may ski a run called Malifies. The summit is two thousand meters. Down below is the Matukituki Valley—rich green farmlands dotted with sheep, deer, and the Matukituki River, which flows into Lake Wanaka. We stop about a thousand meters above the valley and are picked up. As the helicopter zooms off above the sheep, it's a very New Zealand moment."

As mentioned above, the Squirrels don't need a lot of room to touch down. This can open up some interesting terrain, as Mark explained. "Last winter, I had a professional skier and a helicopter pilot skiing with me. In front of us, there was a sharp mountaintop. As we're approaching the peak, I heard the skier say to the pilot, 'We're not going to land on that, are we?' The pilot replied, 'Hell no.' We proceeded to land right at the top. They didn't have much to say but their smiles showed their thoughts.

"I think they were impressed."

MARK SEDON has been a full-time, internationally qualified (IFMGA) climbing and ski guide for twelve years. He has guided over a dozen Himalayan expeditions including summiting Mount Everest. Mark has also guided six expeditions to date to Antarctica including two ski expeditions. He's guided in Europe, Alaska, South America, Indonesia, and extensively in New Zealand. He also has led several Northern Hemisphere winter ski experiences in places like Utah (four winters), Canada (one), Japan (one) and Austria (two). He is a respected avalanche forecaster and teaches courses to students varying in experience from beginner to experienced guides. He is an approachable, enthusiastic guide who is driven to deliver good-quality, enjoyable skiing that's safe. Mark wrote and supplied photos for his book, *Classic Rock Climbing in New Zealand,* and co-wrote *Adventure Consultant's Climbers Guide.* He now operates Kiwi Ski Guide (www .kiwiskiguide.com) in addition to his work with Harris Mountains Heli-Ski in New Zealand and Kashmir Heli Ski in Gulmarg, India.

If You Go

▶ **Getting There:** Visitors fly into Queenstown, which is served by Air New Zealand (800-262-1234; www.airnewzealand.com) via Auckland and Christchurch.

▶ **Season:** The heli-ski season in the Southern Alps generally runs from July through September. Nearby areas (Coronet and The Remarkables) are open June through October.

▶ **Lift Tickets:** A day of heli-skiing out of Queenstown with Harris Mountain Heli-Ski (www.heliski.co.nz) begins at $845 (NZ).

▶ **Level of Difficulty:** Skiers/riders should be of at least intermediate ability. Guides can take you to terrain that's as challenging as you wish to bite off.

▶ **Accommodations:** Destination Queenstown (+64 3 441 0700; www.queenstown-nz .co.nz) lists lodging options in the Southern Alps's hub town.

LYNGEN ALPS

RECOMMENDED BY **Kelly Holland**

To many, Norway's finest alpine skiing moment may have come in 1994 at Lillehammer, when the town a bit north of Oslo hosted the Winter Olympics. Kelly Holland's finest skiing moment in Norway came almost seven hundred miles north among the fjords of the Lyngen Alps, where few resorts and no gondolas—or even rope tows—awaited her.

"I was in Europe a lot that year, ski racing, as Peak Performance, a Swedish company, was my main sponsor," Kelly recalled. "I was participating in a big competition at Riksgränsen in Sweden, and a photographer friend of mine was planning to go up to northern Norway to do a story on skiing in the midnight sun. A writer friend was scheduled to go along, but he had to cancel at the last minute. As I was already in Scandinavia, I got the opportunity to take his place. My interest was piqued. Getting a chance to ski above the Arctic Circle was unique in itself. Since it was June, we'd have twenty-four-hour sunshine at that latitude, which was always intriguing. When the competition was done, we got in a car and drove north toward the village of Lyngseidet."

Lyngseidet sits on the peninsula of Lyngen in the county of Troms, at the northwest corner of Norway—some two hundred miles above the Arctic Circle (latitude 66.56 degrees, if you're counting). In this part of the world, fingers of land separated by fjords (formed by glaciers) stick out into the Arctic Ocean. Much of the fjordland has spines of mountains that climb from sea level to heights of three, four, or five thousand feet. Clad in snow much of the year, these seaside mountains yield a stunning contrast of bright blue and shimmering white, especially in the season of the Midnight Sun. The Lyngen Alps stretch approximately sixty miles along the western shore of the Lyngen Peninsula; the highest peak here is Store Lenangstind, which tops out at 5,328 feet. Not so terribly high . . . unless you have to skin your way to the top!

OPPOSITE: Midnight (or slightly after midnight) runs can be had in Norway's Lyngen Alps.

DESTINATION

35

"Lyngseidet was a hidden gem," Kelly continued. "We found a little inn that looks out on the fjord. On our first afternoon, we were served shrimp cocktails on the front porch, with the sea in front of us and steep mountains behind. There's not much of a skiing infrastructure around Lyngen. We scoped things out the first day we were in town, speaking to a number of locals, to get a sense of how to make our way around. You can drive around the peninsula pretty easily and scope out lines from the road. The mountains really explode upward right from the water's edge. Eventually, we tracked down a guy named Froda who knew enough to lead us to some spots. We couldn't help but think of *Lord of the Rings.*" (*Note: Since Kelly's visit, several guide services have begun operating around Lyngseidet. Several outfitters offer combination sailing/skiing adventures where you sleep on a live-aboard boat and sail around the fjords from mountain to mountain.*)

Kelly and her companions began their ascent in the early evening. "We put skins on our skis and began following Froda up one of the mountains, not far from our inn," she continued. "It was super shady on that side of the mountain, thus very icy. At one point, I mentioned that I thought we should have crampons; in fact, one member of our party did fall, and slid all the way to the bottom, but fortunately we weren't too far up at that point. After a few hours, we reached a flat ridge that was out of the shade. The snow was nice and soft here. We toured around the ridge for a while. We had magnificent views of the ocean, and the alpenglow was incredible. Though it was almost midnight, the sun was still up, a glowing orange ball low on the horizon. There was plenty of light; it seemed like it was about five P.M. We began looking for a good way down. Froda didn't have too much information to offer on this point. 'I think you'll be okay if you go that way,' he said, pointing to the north. Then he left us.

"We toured over to the north side of the mountain, and found a nice slot. The slot was filled with powder all the way down to the valley. Skiing this amazingly soft snow, enveloped by the glow of the midnight sun, was a pretty magical experience. Eventually, the snow ran out, and we had to hike almost three hours through a valley littered with glacial rocks, in our ski boots. By the time we reached the car, it was six A.M. I would sum it up like this: lots of nasty, icy touring, where at times I felt like I was sliding for my life, then a couple hours of amazing snow with the kind of views you don't get every day."

Kelly's tale from the Lyngen Alps—with its highs and lows—would certainly qualify for a once-in-a-lifetime experience. Another interesting experience—one that she might not be as eager to duplicate—awaited her in town. "Lyngseidet is not a big tourist town, and I was the token American," she recalled. "When we went into a little restaurant for lunch, the proprietress was very excited. She said, 'You must let me make you a whale burger!' I was game for it. She rushed over to get some fresh whale meat at the butcher, and then prepared it. She proudly served it, and I was excited. But it was the worst thing I've ever eaten—and I enjoy meat. I felt very bad that I couldn't finish it after all her efforts, so I wrapped it in a napkin when she wasn't looking and put it in my purse."

KELLY HOLLAND competed on the IFSA World Tour for several years with a couple of top finishes and amazing travels along the way. ("I owe a big thanks to Peak Performance, Oakley Eyewear, Völkl/Tecnica, Lululemon, Alta Ski Resort, and Dakine for all of their help over the years," Kelly said. "And it should not go unsaid that my parents are at the top of my sponsor list . . . they've always been my biggest support.") Before joining the IFSA Tour, she spent a couple of years on the U.S. Development Freestyle Ski Team. Kelly retired from professional skiing in 2008 and earned a BS in nursing from Duke University. She presently practices at a hospital near her home in Bozeman, Montana.

If You Go

► **Getting There:** To reach Lyngseidet, you'll want to fly to Tromsø, which is served by SAS (800-221-2350; www.flysas.com) and Norwegian (+47 2149 00 15; www.norwegian .com). Lyngseidet is about forty miles west of Tromsø by car or bus.

► **Season:** The season in the Lyngen Alps runs from February through June.

► **Lift Tickets:** No tickets are needed (as there are no lifts). If you choose to embark on a guided tour, a week's trip (which includes lodging, meals, transportation to ski locales, and mountain guides) from Lyngen Lodge (www.lyngenlodge.com) runs 25,500 Norwegian Kroner (around $4,500). Mountain Spirit Guides (www.mountain-spirit-guides.com) also offers guided trips from a base lodge or a sailboat.

► **Level of Difficulty:** Guided trips can be tailored for skiers of intermediate ability (and superior fitness), but only advanced skiers should consider do-it-yourself ventures.

► **Accommodations:** Options around the Lyngen Peninsula are highlighted at www .lyngenalp.no. Some will day trip up from Tromsø (www.visittromso.no), which is a sizable city.

DESTINATION

35

MT. BACHELOR

RECOMMENDED BY **Mike Adams**

"I understand the appeal of marquee ski areas," Mike Adams began, "but I really appreciate the thrill of having a wonderful ski experience at a lesser-known resort. I've had some
unbelievable days at such venues. One such spot is Mt. Bachelor, in central Oregon. It's
special to me in several ways. First of all, you're skiing on a volcano. How many times can
you say that you've skied on a volcano? Thanks to Bachelor's conical shape, you have skiable terrain from the summit wherever you turn—360 degrees of skiing. You don't always
have the best weather at Bachelor, and there are times when the summit is closed to skiing. But when it clears and conditions are right, skiing off the Summit Lift can give you
access to unbelievable, untracked terrain."

Mt. Bachelor rests near the center of Oregon's Cascade Mountains, some twenty miles
west of the city of Bend. Though it's on the eastern (that is, dryer) side of the range,
Bachelor sees, on average, almost four hundred inches of snow each year. Bachelor is a
young mountain; geologists estimate that it was formed between eleven thousand and fifteen thousand years ago; it's believed to have last erupted some eight thousand years ago.
(No seismic activity has been recorded in modern times.) It takes its name from its "aloof"
position relative to a nearby group of iconic mountains, the Three Sisters. The first modest
ski operation on the mountain was opened in 1941; at the same time, a training camp for
combat engineers was established nearby on the site of what would become the resort
community of Sunriver. By 1958, a more formal operation opened as Bachelor Butte. By
1983, the areas had been rebranded as Mt. Bachelor, as operators feared that the name
"Bachelor Butte" did not reflect a ski area of substance. The name was officially changed
on Oregon's maps, and Mt. Bachelor expanded to include over 3,600 acres of inbounds
terrain, with a vertical drop of 3,365 feet—a mountain by almost anyone's standards.

OPPOSITE:
Mt. Bachelor
doesn't always
deliver great
snow—but when
it does, it's
really great.

DESTINATION

36

"I first visited Bachelor in 1997, when I moved to Portland after Adidas had acquired Salomon," Mike continued. "My sons Cameron and Kieran were ski racers at the time, and they had a great program over at Bachelor. [Thanks to its long season, Bachelor is a regular training ground for the U.S. Ski Association and many Olympians and professional athletes.] We'd drive over from Portland (about four hours) whenever we could, and we got to know a lot of locals. One skier, Mark Ford (who raced for Colorado University in the early seventies) shared a lot of his local knowledge."

As Mike mentioned above, skiers and boarders at Bachelor can run 360 degrees from the summit. The dormant volcano, which has seventy-one trails, is oriented in two halves, Frontside (east-facing) and Backside (west-facing). The front is given over primarily to beginner and intermediate trails; the back is entirely expert terrain and where Mike has found most of his best Bachelor adventures. "There's some very memorable terrain on the back, when the conditions are right. Larry Valley, Curly, and Smokey Bowl come to mind. In some spots, you're skiing in sluices created by lava flows, not like anything I've seen anywhere else. They're little canyons, almost like half-pipes. On the edges of these canyons there's rock, but snow blows into the interior, and the powder can be unbelievable. There are other curiosities, too. There are sinkholes that you'll encounter from time to time, almost like vent holes. I saw kids fall in a few times, and then climb out."

If you happen to get lost among the mountain's 3,683 acres, look for one of the folks in the red jackets—these are Mt. Bachelor Ambassadors, and they're on the hill to help you get oriented and have a good time. For boarders, Mt. Bachelor also offers terrain parks, including an Olympic-size super pipe; it's been ranked among the top five snowboard resorts in North America by readers of TransWorld Snowboarding.

Part of the appeal of skiing and boarding at Bachelor is the chance to enjoy the unique landscape of central Oregon and the vibe of Bend. Here the pinyon pine– and sagebrush-dotted high-desert country that characterizes much of eastern Oregon meets the Cascades, which protect greater Bend from western Oregon's infamous precipitation, yielding nearly three hundred days of sunshine a year. "One of the beauties of the area is that you're not in winter until you get to four thousand feet," Mike added. "If you want to mix snow sports with other activities, you can usually do so." These activities might include trout fishing on one of four local rivers; golf on one of twenty-five area courses; rock climbing on nearby Smith Rock; and in the spring, kayaking and whitewater rafting. Bend, a former lumber town, has emerged as an epicenter for outdoor recreation. In addition to fine restaurants and sweeping Cascades views, Bend is a beer connoisseurs' paradise, with ten craft breweries/brewpubs (as of this writing). Visitors can tour the brewpubs on the Bend Ale Trail via the Cycle Pub, a sixteen-person pedal-powered contraption.

Given the eclectic nature of Mt. Bachelor's Backside terrain, it's no surprise that one of Mike's most precious Bachelor memories involves a run in this region. "I was skiing with my wife, Ellen, who was once captain of the Middlebury Ski Team," he recalled. "We came off Summit Lift, and traversed a bit to the right, and dropped into the Larry Valley area, at the edge of the western side of the mountain. We meandered down to a place we'd never skied; all of a sudden, we were on the border of a canyon. It was all fall line as far as we could see, no one had been there, and no one was around. We skied down side by side. Toward the bottom we stopped and looked back after eighty or ninety turns, and then simultaneously started giggling."

MIKE ADAMS is vice president and commercial director for Amer Sports Winter Sports Equipment in the United States, which includes the Atomic and Salomon brands. His earliest skiing experiences were in Michigan, but through high school, college, and his ski industry career Mike has included New England, Colorado, Oregon, and Utah on his résumé of great places to live and ski.

If You Go

► **Getting There:** Visitors to Mt. Bachelor can fly into nearby Redmond, Oregon, which is served by Alaska Airlines (800-252-7522; www.alaskaair.com) and Delta Airlines (800-221-1212; www.delta.com). Portland (a four-hour drive) is served by most major carriers.

► **Season:** Mt. Bachelor is generally open from Thanksgiving to late May.

► **Lift Tickets:** Day tickets are $76; multi-day tickets are available. See details at www.mtbachelor.com.

► **Level of Difficulty:** Mt. Bachelor has a broad array of terrain, classified as follows: 15 percent novice; 25 percent intermediate; 35 percent advanced; 25 percent expert.

► **Accommodations:** There's no lodging at Mt. Bachelor. Visitors generally stay at the nearby resort community of Sunriver (800-801-8765; www.sunriver-resort.com) or in the city of Bend (877-245-8484; www.visitbend.com).

THE WALLOWAS

RECOMMENDED BY **Kevin Wright**

"Back in 2005, my wife, Kelly, and I decided to move from Colorado to Oregon," Kevin Wright said. "I was a little sad about leaving the big peaks of the Rockies, but comforted myself with the idea that I'd be coming to a place that had good fly-fishing. I wasn't in Oregon long before I traveled out to the eastern part of the state. I was shocked to discover the Wallowa Mountains and the town of Joseph. Here were these tremendous peaks rising in the middle of this very remote wilderness area, and an unspoiled little town. After spending years around mountain towns in my work in the ski industry, Joseph and the Wallowas were like a breath of fresh air. There's a bumper sticker that you see around the area that pretty well sums things up: THESE ARE THE GOOD OLD DAYS."

OPPOSITE: Skiers and riders have to earn their turns in the Wallowas, Oregon's other mountain range.

Pioneers who came upon the Wallowas in the nineteenth century, as they crossed to the south on the Oregon Trail, were awed by the beauty of the mountains, which rise abruptly from the valley of the same name. Parallels were soon drawn to far-distant mountains—today, they are sometimes called "Oregon's Alps" or "Little Switzerland of America." (Wallowa, incidentally, is a Nez Perce name for a fish trap used on local rivers to catch salmon and trout.) The Wallowas sit in the midst of the Eagle Cap Wilderness, which encompasses 565 square miles of granite peaks, alpine lakes, and meadows and glacial valleys. The highest point, Sacajawea Peak, reaches 9,845 feet; thirty other summits are more than eight thousand feet. The Wallowas see some four hundred inches of snow each year—light, dry powder that's not frequently associated with Oregon. This area in the state's northeastern corner, some three-hundred-odd miles east of Portland, is a far cry from the land of giant Douglas firs and coastal sea stacks that many associate with the region. It's wild, wide-open country. And the sense of remoteness one experiences in the Wallowas is only enhanced by the off-the-grid backcountry accommodations favored by fortunate skiers/boarders.

"The ski program in the Wallowas is based around little yurt villages that outfitters have gotten permission to set up seasonally in the wilderness area," Kevin continued. "I stayed at one of the original sites in a spot called McCully Basin." Today's camp, which sits at an elevation of 7,500 feet, consists of four yurts, engineered by Wallowa Alpine Huts owner and "yurtmeister" Connelly Brown. (A yurt, if you're unfamiliar with the term, is a portable, circular structure with a wooden frame, and cloth stretched over the frame—think roomier and more substantial than a tent, less permanent than a cabin.) It's about a four-mile skin through thick forests into the yurts at McCully, with sojourners gaining 1,800 feet of elevation along the way; boarders are provided with snowshoes. Once you arrive on the morning of day one, you drop off your extra clothing and get ready to "earn your turns." There's a variety of terrain to choose from: wide open bowls, couloirs, and old-growth glades.

"The guides are outdoor junkies, and their enthusiasm really adds to the overall experience," Kevin said. "At the beginning of the trip, they try to determine what you want to accomplish: Ski powder? Hone your avalanche skills? The guides do their best to accommodate you. You might spend all day getting to one or two spots for a few epic runs, or you can stay closer to camp and get in a number of shorter runs. I'd say that on my trip, we got in about ten thousand feet vertical a day—and you're pretty whooped by the end of it. A nice thing about the McCully Basin camp is that you can ski pretty late. Everything funnels back into the yurt zone. Once you're back in camp, you can have a sauna and settle in with a libation. If the group desires, the guides can even bring in a keg of beer from Terminal Gravity, one of the great local breweries. They kill you with the food—though you've earned it. Most of the meat and produce is locally sourced. When everyone is done eating, the guides scrape all the leftovers into a big dog bowl. They then call in one of the Bernese mountain dogs that are part of the team. The dog will eat it all. It's kind of disgusting in a beautiful way."

McCully Basin is one of four camps visitors can skin/snowshoe into. There's also the Big Sheep camp, which lies one drainage beyond McCully and features some prime glade skiing habitat. (It's possible to combine a stay at McCully with a few nights at Big Sheep.) To the south, there are two newer campsites, Norway Basin and Schnieder Cabin. "The terrain is so unexplored in this part of the Wallowas," Kevin added, "they're still skiing unnamed runs. It's rare to have such an experience in the Lower 48."

The town of Joseph, at the base of the Wallowas, takes its name from Chief Joseph, leader of the Wallowa band of the Nez Perce. In addition to being the jumping-off point for outdoors people exploring the Eagle Cap Wilderness, Joseph has earned a national reputation for its bronze foundries and galleries. Some of the nation's most highly acclaimed artists cast their bronzes at one of the four area foundries or show their work in one of the many galleries that line the town's picturesque Main Street. Seven permanent sculptures are on display, including one of Chief Joseph.

KEVIN WRIGHT hails from Upstate New York. His steady migration west began with a move to Colorado in 1996, where he worked in the ski industry and married his wife, Kelly. In search of a new adventure and a progressive city close to as many outdoor recreational opportunities as possible, Kevin, Kelly, and their two black Labs moved to Portland in 2005. Kevin spends as much time as he can get away with outside, mountain biking, skiing, fishing, and hiking. Today, he is the vice president of global marketing at Travel Oregon, but you are likely to find him on one of Oregon's many rivers, trails, or mountains with his two children, Gus and Edie.

If You Go

▶ **Getting There:** The towns of Joseph and Halfway are the jumping-off points for Wallowa adventures. They're each roughly six hours east of Portland.

▶ **Season:** Wallowa backcountry skiing generally runs from mid-December through mid-April.

▶ **Lift Tickets:** Several guides lead skiers into the Wallowas, including Wallowa Alpine Huts (541-398-1980; www.wallowahuts.com) and Wing Ridge Ski Tours (541-398-1980; www.wingski.com). Three days of skiing/two nights' lodging trips begin at $550.

▶ **Level of Difficulty:** Guests should be in good physical shape, as you must "earn your turns." Terrain is mostly expert-oriented, though guides can often accommodate intermediates.

▶ **Accommodations:** You'll find a list of options for before/after your backcountry trip in Joseph/Halfway at www.wallowahuts.com.

DESTINATION

37

LE MASSIF

RECOMMENDED BY **Leslie Anthony**

"I grew up in Toronto, where the skiing was not much to write home about," Leslie Anthony began. "There were some small hills in the region and nothing you could describe as powder. In the lift lines, you'd sometimes hear people whispering about this place in Quebec called Le Massif. The whisperers said there was no lift, but school buses would take you to the top of a large mountain. Once there, you had guides and skied fresh powder. This made little sense to me, as it didn't square with what I knew of eastern skiing. I couldn't imagine a place where there was enough snowfall to support powder skiing, let alone a big mountain with powder."

Le Massif rises near the center of the Charlevoix region, roughly fifty miles northeast of Quebec City. At a height of less than 2,700 feet, the mountain might be easily dismissed; yet nearly all the mountain's 2,645 feet translate into vertical (namely 2,526 feet). This gives Le Massif more vertical than any mountain east of the Canadian Rockies. Perhaps more importantly, the mountain's location on the north shore of the St. Lawrence River generates Rockies-like snowfalls—some years, more than twenty feet.

"By the time I'd reached my early twenties, I'd had a chance to ski-bum around a bit," Leslie continued. "I'd spent time in South America, New Zealand, skied a few volcanoes in Mexico. This was the early 1980s, and many people were learning to telemark and do more backcountry skiing, trying to find fresh powder. I was hanging out with the telemark crowd in Ontario, an adventurous group. Though I'd traveled halfway around the world to ski, I still hadn't made it to Le Massif. Then an opportunity arose. I was beginning to do some writing, and I was invited to go over as a guest of a Quebec tourism group. I jumped on the chance with a photographer named Henry Georgi. I found that all the rumors were true—but the mountain was bigger and better than I'd heard.

OPPOSITE: Le Massif's impressive vertical and its perch above the St. Lawrence River make it unique in eastern North America.

"We arrived on St. Patrick's Day, and were greeted by sixty centimeters (two feet) of snow—as much as I'd seen in Ontario in ten years! The guys who'd started the ski operation—Marc Deschamps and Jean Chouinard—were extremely passionate about skiing the Charlevoix region and assembling a downhill experience you couldn't have anywhere else. Deschamps had built a road from the highway up to the escarpment. He'd contracted with local ski buses to ferry skiers from the bottom to the top. There were nine buses total, which could accommodate three hundred skiers. He would never sell more tickets than that. It was a half-hour ride. Each bus had two guides. They'd get everyone singing songs on the ride up, tell jokes, hand out cookies—it was utterly unique.

"At that time, none of the runs had names, just numbers. Some went all the way down to sea level; there was a little village at the bottom. That day, we made five runs. It was all untracked powder. The vistas were otherworldly, as the mountain looks out over the St. Lawrence River, which is twenty-five miles across. We could see icebergs in the river, and could look out all the way to Maine, fifty or sixty miles to the south. The vertical was so precipitous, at times you felt like you were going to ski into the water.

"The photos Henri took that trip were out of this world. Le Massif looked like a B.C. heli-ski operation. The images made their way to Casey Sheehan at *Powder*, and he asked if there was anything he should know about the operation. I wrote a story, and they went nuts, as they'd never had anything like this from the east. Soon I was one of their main contributors, and my career as a ski journalist was launched."

There have been changes at Le Massif since Leslie's first visit. School buses have been replaced by high-speed ski lifts. A train from Quebec City now delivers visitors to the base of the mountain, a well-appointed lodge waits at the top, and restaurants showcasing the bounties of greater Charlevoix are dotted about the terrain. Many of these amenities come courtesy of Daniel Gauthier, cofounder of Cirque du Soleil, who acquired the resort in 2002. Gauthier has also been sprinkling Vaudeville-style entertainers around the mountain—jugglers, ice sculptors, clowns, and the like—who add a new dimension of entertainment. "I've tracked the evolution of Le Massif from its humble beginnings," Leslie said. "It's so different now from the backwoods experience it once was, with the wild guides leading sing-alongs on the bus. It's a pretty slick operation now, but I think it's still true to the vision that its founders had to create a low-impact ski area.

"From a skiing perspective, I think they've continued to cultivate a culture where people can do any kind of skiing they want to. They still have some of the steepest and longest runs in the east. They have some massive backcountry terrain with gulleys and trees. There's even an FIS-sanctioned Olympic downhill run [La Charlevoix, with a pitch of 64 percent in places], and an Alps-style luge run that runs five or six miles. I don't think you'd find that sort of thing in the states, due to liability issues."

One thing hasn't changed—the unmatched Gulf of St. Lawrence views. "You can't get views like this anywhere else in North America," Leslie added, "and that in itself is uplifting. If you're on top of an icy hill in Vermont, it's hard to get past figuring out how to get down. On Le Massif, you're unconcerned about how you get down, even if you have crummy conditions. You're taking in what's in front of you, not what's underfoot."

LESLIE ANTHONY is a writer, editor, and filmmaker. His PhD in zoology belies a career that includes managing editor of *Powder* and creative director of *Skier*. He resides on the masthead of several North American ski and outdoor magazines, and his work appears annually in twelve countries in seven languages. He writes broadly on subjects ranging from imaginary monsters to fossil smuggling, invasive species to China's nascent ski industry. He has authored several books, including the acclaimed *White Planet: A Mad Dash Through Modern Global Ski Culture*.

If You Go

▶ **Getting There:** Quebec City is the staging area for Le Massif, and it's served by many carriers, including Air Canada (888-247-2262; www.aircanada.ca) and Delta Airlines (800-241-4141; www.delta.com). Train service from Quebec City is available from VIA Rail (888-842-7245; www.viarail.ca).

▶ **Season:** The season at Le Massif generally runs from early December to late April. See up-to-date ski reports at www.lemassif.com (877-536-2774).

▶ **Lift Tickets:** Full-day tickets are $67 (CAD). Multi-day tickets are available.

▶ **Level of Difficulty:** Roughly half of Le Massif's fifty-plus trails and glades are classified as beginner and intermediate; 35 percent of the mountain's terrain is considered expert.

▶ **Accommodations:** A number of ski and stay packages are available. See details at www.lemassif.com/en/planifier/forfaits.

DESTINATION

38

MONT-TREMBLANT

RECOMMENDED BY **Eric Gagne**

You may not be able to escape to Chamonix at a moment's notice. But if you live in North America and have a hankering for a distinctly French-flavored alpine experience, point your compass northwest of Montreal and head to Mont-Tremblant.

"Mont-Tremblant has some challenging runs and great acreage," Eric Gagne began, "but you're not going to find the big-mountain skiing that you might encounter in the Rockies or the Alps. What you will find, however, is a total experience that's very pleasing. Visitors who aren't French speakers really appreciate the Quebecois atmosphere, which has an exotic feeling; it's like visiting Europe without going abroad. The European feeling is enhanced by the pedestrian village at the base of the mountain, and the beautiful architecture of the structures. Here in Quebec, we can't always rely on Mother Nature providing all the snow we'd like to see. Luckily, we have one of the most powerful snowmaking systems in the east, so we can give visitors nice coverage. There's also a strong grooming program in place. For skiers who enjoy a carpet, we can provide it."

Mont-Tremblant (elevation 2,871 feet) rests in the Laurentian Mountains in southern Quebec, eighty miles northwest of Montreal. The Algonquin Indians called it Manitonga Soutana, or "Mountain of the Spirits." These First Nation people believed that anytime someone broke the laws of nature or broke the peace, the spirits would make the mountain tremble . . . hence *tremblant*. Like so many European ski destinations, Mont-Tremblant was first developed as a summer retreat, in this case for urbanites in Montreal and Ottawa City seeking cool mountain air. Development was facilitated by the construction of a train line, the P'tit Train du Nord (Little Train of the North), in 1892.

It was American millionaire Joseph Bondurant Ryan who recognized the mountain's potential as a ski resort. Ryan was introduced to the area, then a wilderness region, by a

OPPOSITE: A special facet of the Mont-Tremblant experience is its European-style village.

DESTINATION

39

friend, the acclaimed broadcaster Lowell Thomas, in the mid-1930s. The two men climbed Mont-Tremblant on skis, hoping to take in the view across the Laurentians. At the summit, Ryan is alleged to have said, "This has to be the most beautiful sight in the world. There is only one thing wrong. It is too difficult getting up here. I believe I'll fix that!" Ryan's "fix" was to buy the mountain. Initially, the province of Quebec, which owned the property, was resistant to the idea. Ryan eventually called in a favor from Ben Smith, a powerful Wall Street broker, who placed a call to Quebec's premier, and the deal went through. Ryan was given two years to develop his fledgling property, or risk forfeiture. Working frantically, he was able to meet the deadline, cutting trails for twenty runs, installing lifts, building roads into the property, and constructing the twenty buildings that would make up the village. Mont-Tremblant opened in February 1939.

Mont-Tremblant is consistently ranked among the best eastern skiing North America has to offer. This is in part thanks to the resort's aforementioned snowmaking system—a thousand snow guns working to provide coverage on 465 out of 654 acres—and to the mountain's great variety of terrain, enough to make novices feel comfortable and experts interested. Mont-Tremblant offers forty-nine miles of trails, spread over four sectors: North Side (Versant Nord), South Side (Versant Sud), Sunny Side (Versant Soleil), and The Edge (Versant Edge). Eric shared a few favorites. "On the North Side, there's a beginner's trail called Le Petit Bonheur (The Little Joy), which is named for a famous song by a beloved Quebec artist, Félix LeClerc. It's a real joy to go down. For the expert skier on the North Side, I like Devil's River and a little pass off that trail called Boiling Kettle. Devil's River follows the natural terrain; there's no snowmaking. Boiling Kettle is a steep pitch with big moguls. You need a lot of snow to go there. On the South Side, there's some great expert terrain. I'm a former World Cup skier, and I can find good turns and challenges here. Ryan and Lower Ryan—named for Mont-Tremblant's founder—are not to be missed. Three other famous runs are Zig-Zag, Vertige, and Grand Prix. There's a little pass off Grand Prix where you get a magnificent view of Mont-Tremblant Lake and the whole region. The Edge has good glade terrain for experts.

"If you find yourself on Versant Soleil around lunchtime, you can't miss a stop at Le Refuge. It's a little log cabin set among the trees, about a quarter of the way down. The cabin is very typical of old Quebecois culture. There's no plumbing, no electricity; if you have to use the bathroom, there's an outhouse. The people who run the place bring everything in by snowmobile. They serve soups, sandwiches, and little snacks. It's a very quaint spot and speaks to the Mont-Tremblant experience."

Having skied at Mont-Tremblant for more than forty years, Eric has many fond memories. Most involve sharing the mountain with friends. "I remember a magical March 23 from a few years back," he recalled. "It was a big powder day—we had forty to fifty centimeters of fresh snow on the ground. I was approaching the gondola, and I ran into my best friend. It was his birthday, and he'd decided to spend it on the mountain. We hadn't planned on meeting, we just happened to be heading up at the same time. We spent the whole day riding the powder, tearing ourselves up, burning all the fuel we had."

ERIC GAGNE has ancestral land near Tremblant, and his grandparents founded the La Conception region. It was no surprise that he came back during winter ski season and never left. Eric has been working for Station Mont-Tremblant for almost twenty years as a sales representative and a volume distributor for ski and golf tickets for a corporations network. A former member of Canada's national ski team (in telemarking), he participated in two World Cup series in that field in 2005/6 and 2006/7. Eric is part of Tremblant's new generation, and will definitely be a part of its history.

If You Go

▶ **Getting There:** Mont-Tremblant is 1.5 hours from Montreal, which is served by most major carriers. Porter Airlines (888-619-8622; www.flyporter.com) offers direct service to Mont-Tremblant from Newark and Toronto.

▶ **Season:** Mont-Tremblant opens in late November and generally remains open until mid-April, though some seasons extend into May.

▶ **Lift Tickets:** Adult day passes are $76 (CAD); a variety of packages are outlined at www.tremblant.ca.

▶ **Level of Difficulty:** Mont-Tremblant's ninety-four trails are categorized as 17 percent beginner; 33 percent intermediate; 50 percent expert.

▶ **Accommodations:** Mont-Tremblant offers a host of lodging options. For details, call 888-738-1777 or visit www.tremblant.ca.

DESTINATION

39

KAMCHATKA

RECOMMENDED BY **James Morland**

Kamchatka—a place that may be best known as a minor outpost on the Risk game board than a heli-ski destination—is one of the world's last great uninhabited wildernesses. This peninsula adjoining the far eastern reaches of Russia is comparable in size to Japan (which lies to the south), and is bordered by the Pacific, the Bering Sea, and the Sea of Okhotsk. Kamchatka is home to the world's largest population of brown bears (i.e., grizzlies), some of the healthiest salmon populations in existence, and 160 volcanoes—a number of which make for one of the world's more exotic downhill experiences.

OPPOSITE: The sea is never far away when you're exploring the volcanic mountains of Kamchatka.

"The first thing I say to people who are considering a trip to Kamchatka is that the snow conditions are not always perfect powder," James Morland began. "But I'm always quick to add that even if you have poor conditions, it will still be one of the most incredible ski/snowboard trips of your life. No one—not even Russian tourists—was allowed to visit until the early 1990s, as Kamchatka was classified as a strategic military zone. Tourism is still a new concept there, and visitors somewhat of a novelty. People are very interested in talking to you—even though you can't understand what they are saying half the time! It's a really sparsely populated part of the world. In fact, the peninsula is the size of Germany, Austria, and Switzerland combined, and there are less than 400,000 residents . . . and 250,000 of them are in the city of Petropavlovsk. It's about as wild and remote a region as you can find anywhere. On a scenery scale, it's simply spectacular. You're skiing on active volcanoes, sometimes into the crater, sometimes right down to the beach. Kamchatka also has some of the world's longest runs. One run here is like several normal heli-ski runs stacked up on each other. They seem to go on forever."

Petropavlovsk is the starting point for heli-ski adventures in Kamchatka. It's safe to say that its architecture—monotonous, Soviet-style structures in vogue circa 1948—does

DESTINATION

40

not rival that of St. Petersburg. Even locals joke about the city's lack of charm. "Petropavlovsk is a grim city, but its ugliness is offset by the friendliness of the residents and the awesome spectacle of the landscapes that surround it," James continued. "We used to base ourselves in town, but now we stay about forty minutes outside of town in Paratunka, known as the hot-spring valley. Here, the helicopter—an Mi-8—can land right next to the hotel. Communication at the hotel, and anywhere else around Kamchatka, for that matter, is an amusing aspect of the trip. When you sit down to breakfast or dinner, you might order one thing and have something completely different show up. Suffice it to say, there's not a particularly strong customer service mentality. Rather than getting angry about this, guests will do well to take it as part and parcel of the experience." You're much more likely to find iced vodka than Chardonnay served with dinner. "There will likely be some Russian visitors at the dinner table," James added. "Trying to keep up with them on the vodka toasts can be dangerous. During May trips, the helicopters sometimes don't take off until ten A.M., when the snow has softened—but we've still had cases of Western guests not making it aboard, thanks to the night before."

The Mi-8s are powerful helicopters capable of carrying a passel of Alpinists. "It can fit in twelve skiers and four guides, plus two pilots, plus all the skis," James described. "It can also cover a lot of ground. Flying from Paratunka, we'll sometimes be in the air thirty minutes before we touch down on a volcanic peak. Depending on the terrain, we'll either split into two groups or ski in one larger group. Either way, it's one of the few heli-ski venues I've visited where, instead of stepping straight into their bindings and skiing straight away, visitors stand around with their jaws hanging open, cameras out, trying to take in the immensity of what's in front of them. I remember one landing where we were surrounded by snow-covered mountains, while in the distance there was a peak that was jet-black. It was covered in ash and smoking away. We're never far from the ocean. In some places the water is protected from the wind and thus calm, and you can see the mountains brilliantly reflected."

Given its peninsular locale just east of Siberia, it's not surprising that Kamchatka can see a bit of weather, including some wind . . . well, a lot of wind. "On my first visit, it was evident that there had been a ferocious wind," James recalled. "Every single aspect looked like solid concrete! Amazingly, we still managed to find plenty of good powder, and in between we skied some exceptional spring snow: some sparkling surface hoar; cold, dry, chalky snow; sun crust; wind crust; rimed boilerplate; and everything in between. You name it, we skied it. All in all, the vast majority of runs were on very good snow. The terrain varies greatly from one area to another, with some good tree skiing at lower elevations, big volcanic faces, long steep couloirs, wide-open bowls, and long, mellow cruisers. A lot of these runs end with a mile or two of relatively low-angle terrain as you head toward the beach. You don't need to turn; you can just sit back, relax, and check out the scenery—a smoking volcano over one shoulder, a steaming geyser over the other, and the deep blue sea before you. Usually, you'll get in at least four runs before lunch. The average run will go about four thousand vertical feet, though some will go nearly ten thousand feet. After a lunch of hot soup, sandwiches—and of course, vodka—you'll have a few more runs and usually end the day by skiing down to some hot springs near the beach. There you can toast the day with a glass or two of Russian champagne (or vodka) as the surf breaks in the background."

JAMES MORLAND has been involved in the front line of the ski industry for fifteen years, and started EA Heliskiing (www.eaheliskiing.com) in the late 1990s. Since then he has been involved in all aspects of running the business, right down to the grass roots of guiding. James is a member of the Association of Canadian Mountain Guides and is partway through the UIAGM guide certification in Canada. He has a particular interest in snow safety and holds the Canadian Avalanche Association's (CAA) level 2 certification. James has also been a professional yacht skipper for twelve years, and has taken guests sailing all around the world, from Alaska to Southeast Asia.

If You Go

▶ **Getting There:** The trip described above is run out of Petropavlovsk, which is served by Aeroflot (888-686-4949; www.aeroflot.ru) via Moscow.

▶ **Season:** Most heli-ski trips to Kamchatka are led in April and May.

▶ **Lift Tickets:** A week's worth of heli-skiing with EA Heliskiing (+44 203 059 8787; www.eaheliskiing.com) out of Petropavlovsk runs around 7,000 euros.

▶ **Level of Difficulty:** Kamchatka is recommended for advanced skiers only.

▶ **Accommodations:** Lodging is provided at Hotel Antarius in Paratunka.

DESTINATION

40

KRASNAYA POLYANA

RECOMMENDED BY **Thibaud Duchosal**

"A few years ago, I met some Russians on a ski trip in the Ukraine," Thibaud Duchosal recalled, "and they said, 'You have to come to Russia to ski.' I like seeing new places, so I went. On my first trip, I went to Mount Elbrus, which is the tallest mountain in the Caucasus [at 18,510 feet]. It's a huge mountain, very wild and amazing for skiing. However, the people there were very unfriendly, and I didn't feel especially safe in the streets. Some people I met there said I should try Krasnaya Polyana. I came the next year on the Freeride World Tour. There wasn't much of a skiing infrastructure. There were only a couple resorts, and not a huge amount of vertical relative to some places—maybe 5,000 feet. But that first visit, it snowed almost ten feet over ten days—light, dry powder. It was a paradise. When you visit a place and get such conditions, you have to go back."

Krasnaya Polyana may not roll off the tongue quite so readily as Aspen or St. Anton when your friends are rattling off marquee ski areas, but that may change soon. The resorts here—primarily Rosa Khutor—will host the alpine skiing events in the 2014 Sochi Winter Olympics. Krasnaya Polyana sits in the western Caucasus Mountains in the far southwestern corner of the Russian Federation, fifty miles east of the Black Sea resort town of Sochi and just north of the border with the former Soviet satellite nation Georgia. The Caucasus stretch from the Black Sea to the Caspian Sea, and comprise one of the physical—and certainly psychological—borders between Europe and Asia. A number of peaks in the range eclipse sixteen thousand feet, though the summits around Krasnaya Polyana are in the six thousand– to nine thousand–foot range. "At Rosa Khutor, the experience is about the snow," Thibaud continued. The bad weather rolls in incredibly fast from the Black Sea, and the quality and quantity of the snow is amazing. Every time I've gone, there's been a minimum of five feet; one week, there was thirteen feet of snow.

OPPOSITE:
If Olympic attention brings the crowds to Krasnaya Polyana, heli-ski operators can spirit you to the mountains just north of the resort for fresh tracks.

DESTINATION

41

"In my opinion, the best terrain at Rosa Khutor is in the trees. The forest area is steep and fairly open, and it really gathers snow, though the rules for going off-piste are somewhat arbitrary. In Europe, if you want to go off-piste, you go at your own risk. In Russia, there are no ropes, but access to off-piste areas is closely controlled. There will be times when the conditions are great and the weather is clear, but they won't let you go. Other times when the conditions are dangerous, they open up the off-piste areas. I've tried to understand their thinking, but I can't. At the end of the day, you ski wherever they want you to ski."

The rather autocratic dictates that determine ski policy around greater Krasnaya Polyana are also largely responsible for the significant development that's underway in the region, the development that may put the town on the international ski destination map. It turns out that President, then Prime Minister, and now again President Vladimir Putin is a passionate skier, and that Krasnaya Polyana is one of his favorite resorts. This—and the fact that President Putin recognizes the great public relations potential of a successful Olympic event—will no doubt transform the region. "On my first visit in 2008, there were just a few chairlifts," Thibaud added. "The plan is to have something like fifty chairlifts and much more of the upper mountain served." Four new resorts are under construction in Krasnaya Polyana, all scheduled to be completed before the Games begin. Whether Putin and his counterparts can pull off a Caucasus version of France's Trois Vallees is still to be seen, though Krasnaya Polyana will surely change.

One word of caution: You'll do well to consult your best diplomatic contacts before scheduling a trip to Krasnaya Polyana. If President Putin is present and entertaining guests, the resort may be unceremoniously shut down.

One aspect of the Krasnaya Polyana experience that will likely improve with expansion is the cuisine. "On my earlier visits, the food was typical Russian fare—not very interesting," Thibaud continued. "With the new resorts, they are adding restaurants that feature some European cuisine. Though the food may be better in other places, the people are very warm, and fond of Europeans and Americans. There's definitely a language barrier; no English is spoken. But you can still communicate with your hands and have fun.

"I have good memories from each time I've visited Krasnaya Polyana, and all the memories concern the vast amounts of snow. On my first visit, it snowed twenty inches the night we arrived, and it was still snowing the next morning. My group was thrilled, but some of the Russians we met were unhappy. 'It's a bad day,' they complained. 'It's snowing.' For the next few days, there was no fresh snow. The next evening, it started snowing again, huge flakes the size of pizzas! 'Tomorrow, we're going to have fifty new centimeters,' we said to each other. When we woke up, there was five feet of new snow. All the forest areas were open. It was snowing so hard that even though twenty people had skied down one of the trails below the lifts as we went up, by the time we were going up again, their tracks were covered."

THIBAUD DUCHOSAL was raised in Les Arcs, France. Like all kids in the valley, he started skiing slalom and racing very young, and as an adolescent, turned to freeride and exploring the exceptional terrain that was his backyard. As did his mentors, Enak Gavaggio and the Troubat brothers, Thibaud turned his passion into his profession. Beginning with photo shoots in Scotland and Uzbekistan, he discovered travel and a love of other cultures. He joined film production companies Invert Prod and Garchois Films, and the freeride competitive circuit. The year 2009 was his best thus far, as he finished sixth overall in the World Freeride Tour. Look for Thibaud in Argentina, Russia, the United States, and France, or in the portfolio pages of skiing magazines and a new series of videos, *Eye of the Storm*. Learn more about his adventures at www.thibaud-duchosal.com.

If You Go

► **Getting There:** Krasnaya Polyana is roughly fifty miles east of the Black Sea resort town of Sochi, which is served from Moscow by Aeroflot (888-686-4949; www.aeroflot.ru).

► **Season:** The snow is best from January through mid-March.

► **Lift Tickets:** A day pass at Rosa Khutor is 1,400 rubles (approximately 35 euros). Packages assembled by Big Mountain Trips (888-875-3662; www.bigmountain-trips.com) include flights from Europe to Moscow and Sochi, lodging at three-star hotels, guides, ski passes, and several days of sightseeing in Moscow, and begin at 2,790 euros.

► **Level of Difficulty:** As of this writing, terrain at Rosa Khutor is classified as 59 percent beginner; 6 percent intermediate; 35 percent advanced.

► **Accommodations:** If you choose to go it alone, one acceptable option is the Park Inn at the Rosa Khutor resort (www.parkinn.com/hotel-rosakhutor).

DESTINATION

41

ZERMATT

RECOMMEDED BY **Amadé Perrig**

Since British mountaineer Edward Whymper first summited the Matterhorn—a pyrami-
dal spire that rises nine thousand feet directly above the town of Zermatt, to a height of
14,690 feet—in 1865, alpinists from around the world have flocked here to make their
ascent . . . or simply to stare upon one of the world's most iconic mountains. Many come
today to ski and snowboard at what's become one of the world's largest and most famous
ski centers.

OPPOSITE:
Zermatt is a
sprawling ski
area, connecting
many mountain
hamlets. Here,
the Matterhorn
rises behind the
chapel at Findeln.

"Zermatt is one of the oldest summer and winter resorts in the Alps," Amadé Perrig
began, "but it's interesting to note that, like so many resorts in this area, it got its start as
a summer resort. It's just the opposite of ski area development in the United States,
where many resorts are now trying to appeal to summer visitors. The first hotel opened
here in 1838, and tourism started in earnest over the next few decades, as people came to
hike and climb mountains. Many of the early guests were wealthy English people, and
they could afford to stay in beautiful hotels. Many sprang up to accommodate them.
[Whymper's successful summiting, and the subsequent accident that sent four members
of his party to their death, prompted Queen Victoria to ban mountaineering for British
citizens. This only increased the English appetite for adventure.] Skiing didn't begin in
the Alps until the 1870s. That was in Austria. Though people participated in alpine skiing
around Zermatt at the turn of the century, the first lifts were not built until the late
1920s."

Zermatt rests in the southwest corner of Switzerland, just above the border with Italy;
there are some runs, in fact, where you can ski into Italy, making a visit to Zermatt a truly
international experience! Depending on who you speak to, there are at least three main
ski areas at Zermatt (some identify more discrete areas): the Blauherd/Rothorn area, the

DESTINATION

42

189

Stockhorn/Gornergrat area, and the Klein Matterhorn. While each area has its unique charms from a terrain perspective, they all share four characteristics that help make Zermatt special. "The first is that we're located in the heart of the highest mountains in the Alps," Amadé continued. "There are nine out of the ten highest mountains in Europe here, and thirty-eight peaks over four thousand meters [thirteen thousand feet]. The vistas are dazzling, and the elevation translates into a long season and incredible vertical [over 7,795 feet]. We also have Europe's most beautiful mountain, the Matterhorn, which is in view from so many of our trails. There are so many stories, books, photos, movies, and paintings featuring the Matterhorn. It's part of alpine culture.

"The second reason Zermatt is so special is that it's a car-free place. There's a parking area five miles away; guests take a shuttle train into the village. Not even locals are allowed to drive in the village; we park our cars in a lot that's underground! Without cars, we have no pollution. Zermatt still has an authentic, old alpine village feeling, with houses that are three hundred or four hundred years old. It's like a fairy tale. The streets are narrow, very cozy. Everyone walks, but it's only 1.5 miles from one end of town to the other. Zermatt's wonderful hotel infrastructure is its third special feature. We have 130 lodging options in the village, from top luxury hotels to modest pensiones. All are owned by local people, and many have been in their families for generations. Guests feel very much at home; in fact, 70 percent of the visitors to Zermatt are repeat visitors. We had a gentleman from the United States who came here for one hundred straight years . . . his last visit was at age 104!

"The last reason—but certainly not least—is the fact that Zermatt offers tremendous skiing. There are seventy-three gondolas and ski lifts serving more than one hundred trails that offer more than two hundred miles of skiing/boarding. One big difference between Zermatt—and, for that matter, other Alps resorts—and most U.S. ski areas is that here, every little valley is connected. In the United States, you have certain options to get up to the top, and then you hit boundaries. In the Alps, we ski in all zones, move in the whole arena, including glaciers. There are no boundaries. We have some extremely long trails. One runs eight miles—you ski and ski and ski! (This trail, from the top of Klein, or "Little," Matterhorn to the village of Zermatt, drops 7,250 feet.)

"You will not go hungry on the mountain. There are eighty restaurants scattered about the ski area, many in centuries-old houses. There are also great restaurants at the top of each lift. I would call much of the food gourmet. Our neighbors in Italy, France, Austria, and Germany have many specialties. We've stolen the best from each—but we also have some of our own. These include cheese fondue, served with a crisp white wine, and raclette, which is warmed cheese that's served with boiled onions, potatoes, and pickles. You'll also see air-dried beef and ham served with a dark bread called Roggenbrot. Veal, cut very thin and served with Rösti [which resembles hash browns] is a popular entrée. We have many of our own wines in Switzerland, juicy reds and dry whites. Many visitors say, 'This white wine is great. Why can't we get it in the states?' I joke that we keep it all for ourselves. The Swiss are champions for dessert. The pastries are fantastic."

Amadé Perrig has skied around Zermatt for more than sixty years. He described how a typical morning on the slopes might unfold. "I can step out of my house, take the underground train, and be at the Sunnegga lift in four minutes. My first run, I'd take a trail through the forest, making nice wide turns. I would leave my sunglasses off, so the wind would wash out my eyes. I'd then take a quad up to the Blauherd area, and on up to Rothorn. From there, you can go left or right. There's usually nice powder in there, and morning sunshine. I'd make my way south to Gant and then up to Gornergrat. I might stop and have a little warm-up drink, a schnapps, perhaps. Soon it's time for lunch. There are so many great options, but I like the hamlet of Findeln, near Sunnegga. There are six restaurants there, each one better than the next."

Should you find yourself on Little Matterhorn some winter morning, you may hear an iconic Swiss sound, the sound of yodeling. It's believed that yodeling emerged in the Alps as a means of communication between livestock herders in different villages. For Amadé, it's merely an expression of joy. "When I'm coming down Klein Matterhorn in deep powder, I yodel as I float along," he said. "It echoes off the surrounding hills.

"I like to play golf in the summer, and I used to yodel when I made birdie. But the captain [pro] at the course said I should stop, as I might interrupt someone teeing off."

AMADÉ PERRIG served as the president of tourism in Saas-Fee (Switzerland) and Zermatt (Switzerland) for twenty-five years. As a CEO of Zermatt, he was in charge of the entire resort, which includes more than 70 cable cars, 122 hotels, 7,000 apartments, 300 restaurants, and many sports facilities. He also served as a tourism consultant for planning ski areas in the United States. Amadé was an ardent ski racer in his youth, and is a certified ski instructor; he has climbed his home mountain, the Matterhorn, fifteen times. Amadé is the founder, and was also the president and general secretary, of the European

DESTINATION

42

marketing organization Best of the Alps, which includes the following summer and winter resorts: Garmisch-Partenkirchen (D), Lech (A), Seefeld (A), St. Anton (A), Kitzbühel (A), Cortina d'Ampezzo (I), Chamonix (F), Mégève (F), Davos (CH), Grindelwald (CH), St. Moritz (CH), and Zermatt (CH). He and his wife call Zermatt home, but spend several months in Arizona each year.

If You Go

▶ **Getting There:** Visitors generally fly into Zurich or Geneva (served by most major carriers), and then take a train (operated by the Swiss rail network) to Zermatt. Rail times are three and four hours, respectively.

▶ **Season:** Much of the mountain is open late November to early May. Some areas on the glacier are open year-round.

▶ **Lift Tickets:** Day passes for all the areas in Zermatt run 75 euros. Multi-day passes are available.

▶ **Level of Difficulty:** Zermatt offers a dizzying amount of terrain—some 153 miles of trails—with something for everyone. Terrain is classified as 23 percent beginner; 44 percent intermediate; 33 percent expert.

▶ **Accommodations:** Zermatt Tourismus (+41 27 966 81 00; www.zermatt.ch) highlights the wide range of lodging options in town.

DESTINATION

42

ALTA

RECOMMENDED BY **John Stifter**

John Stifter's relationship with Alta began with some very generous and understanding parents: "When I turned sixteen, my parents offered to take me to a ski area of my choice, within reason, as a birthday gift," he began. "I'd grown up reading *Powder* magazine, and had glorified images of Utah skiing. I was especially enthralled with Alta, thanks in large part to the photography of Lee Cohen. I chose Alta, and some buddies and I headed down from Spokane, where we lived. I still remember driving up Little Cottonwood Canyon with a copy of the *Powder* resort guide and Alta trail maps in my lap. This was before the time of smartphones and WiFi. After everything I'd read and all the photos I'd seen, my expectations were high. They all were exceeded. The snow was softer, the mountain steeper, and to make things even better, as we went to the lift, I saw one of my favorite pro skiers, Kris Ostness, in line. Kris was from Spokane, and my friends and I idolized his ski films. [Kris Ostness appeared on the January 2000 cover of *Powder*, and his films include *Clay Pigeons*, *Tee Time*, and *The Flying Circus*, as well as *Teddybear Crisis*.] When we got to the top of the lift, we skied up to him. 'Are you Kris Ostness? We're from Spokane, and we love your films and skiing.' He smiled and said, 'You want to take a run?' I'll never forget that. Overall, it was a dream come true, just what I expected a Utah ski area to be like."

Alta has been described as a village that happens to have a ski area in the middle, rather than a resort that sprouted a town. Established in 1871 at the upper end of Little Cottonwood Canyon, Alta enjoyed two brief silver booms, the first ending in 1873, the second beginning in early 1904 and lasting until the 1920s. Before the end of the first boom, Alta had three thousand residents! By 1930, the population had declined to six. But several businessmen, skiing Salt Lake City, saw potential in the canyon as a winter playground. Drawing upon Sun Valley, Idaho, as a model, money was raised and a lift was

constructed in Alta, carrying its first passengers skyward in January 1939. As the sport expanded, so did Alta, albeit slowly. By 1970, Alta had 92 full-time residents; by 1990, 397 residents. As word spread about Alta's five-hundred-plus inches of fluffy powder annually and its bountiful terrain, it began to emerge as a top-flight skiing destination.

"Alta has changed a bit over the years," John continued, "but it still has retained much of its original charm, from its lodges to the older lifts and bars. The focus is on skiing, not amenities and massive lodges. It's gotten busier, but there's still a hard-core local scene, and the kind of camaraderie that scene fosters feels like the way skiing *should* be."

Snowboarders, however, are not quite so welcome. The area's tagline, "Alta Is for Skiers," says it all. Alta is certainly not the only mountain to forbid snowboarders from its slopes, but it has been perhaps the most strident. Branding and public relations guru Laura Ries commented on the decision on her blog, *Ries' Pieces*:

> In light of this overwhelming excitement about snowboarding, what did the Alta resort in Utah do? Did they reposition the mountain to attract snowboarders as well as skiers as almost every other ski resort has?

> No, Alta stuck to skiing, said no to snowboarders and according to Alta's website: "Alta is a skier's mountain where snowboarding is not allowed. Alta Ski Area is committed to preserving and protecting the skiing experience."

> Why is this such a brilliant marketing move? Because it does three things:
> 1. The strategy identifies the enemy.
> 2. The strategy preserves a focus.
> 3. The strategy creates controversy.

If you miss snowboarders—or happen to be a boarder who might be seeking terrain with a semblance to Alta—rumor has it that Snowbird, right next door, is open to non-skiers!

John described how an average day might unfold for him at Alta. "There are so many nooks and crannies on the hill, and the guys who ski it all the time can take you into some cool spots. I'll start by cruising up the Collins lift and ski a few High Boy and work the shoulder a bit. It gets tracked out pretty fast, so I'll work my way over to the Wildcat lift

OPPOSITE:
Alta offers ample air as well as well as a seemingly endless supply of "the best snow on earth."

DESTINATION

43

and do a few Keyhole runs at the edge of Snowbird. I'll have lunch—beer and nachos—at the Goldminer's Daughter, which is at the base of the Wildcat and Collins lift. After lunch, I might ride back up Wildcat, ski the fall line under the chair. Then I might head over to the area between the Collins lift and the Sugarloaf lift. From here, you can work both sides. There's lots of traversing here. That acts as a filter to weed the less ambitious skiers out."

Though this is Utah—a place not always noted for its bar life—Alta boasts several watering holes that let visitors cap off the day. "I like the Rustler's Lodge, Goldminer's Daughter, and of course, the Sitzmark Bar in Alta Lodge," John added. "It's been around forever [1939, to be exact, and a perennial top 10 après-ski spot]. Sitting by the roaring fire with a hot-cider drink and everyone smiling with a goggle tan—it's classic."

JOHN STIFTER grew up skiing Schweitzer Mountain Resort in northern Idaho. He free-lanced for ESPN for the Winter X Games and the Honda Ski Tour, during and after his time as a student at Montana State University, before joining *Powder* magazine as associate editor in 2007. In 2012, he was named the magazine's twelfth editor in its forty-one-year history.

If You Go

▶ **Getting There:** Visitors fly into Salt Lake City, which is served by most carriers. From here, it's less than an hour to Alta.

▶ **Season:** Alta generally opens in mid-November and remains open until mid-April, and operates the lifts a bit later in the season on weekends.

▶ **Lift Tickets:** Adult day tickets are $72; multi-day tickets are available.

▶ **Level of Difficulty:** There's a variety of terrain at Alta; trails are rated as 25 percent beginner; 40 percent intermediate; 35 percent advanced.

▶ **Accommodations:** Ski-in/ski-out base lodging, nearby condos, and private homes are available near the mountains. These options are highlighted at www.alta.com. Skiers on a tighter budget may opt to stay in Salt Lake City.

DEER VALLEY RESORT

RECOMMENDED BY **Heidi Voelker**

"I think that there's a myth in the skiing world that people of different abilities can't ski together," Heidi Voelker began. "Deer Valley is the kind of area that dispels that myth. There's something for everyone off of each of the resort's six mountains. Beginners or people getting back on skis are not stuck at the bottom of the mountain. Everyone can get up to the peaks and have a real outdoor experience."

Deer Valley is one of three ski areas in the Wasatch Mountain town of Park City, less than an hour east of Salt Lake City. (Though it may be difficult to fathom, Park City was once considered a ski town before it became known as a movie town with the advent of the Sundance Film Festival.) The first trails at the area were cut by the Works Progress Administration (WPA) in the winter of 1936, as part of a winter carnival sponsored by the Salt Lake City Junior Chamber of Commerce; ten years later, the site became home of Utah's first mechanized lift, using surplus mining equipment and the engine from a Hercules truck. (At this time, it was known as Snow Park; it wouldn't become Deer Valley until 1981.) Today, the resort encompasses six discrete segments spread over six mountains—Little Baldy, Bald Eagle, Bald, Flagstaff, Empire Canyon, and Lady Morgan. Deer Valley doesn't see as much snow as its Cottonwood Canyon counterparts (Alta and Snowbird), but it still averages three hundred inches of The Greatest Snow On Earth®, distributed across one hundred runs and more than two thousand skiable acres. "On powder days, some people will go over to the other areas," Heidi added. "I don't know why. We have so much terrain and relatively few people. On a recent powder day, my group skied until one P.M. before we hit a run that had been tracked."

Since its inception, Deer Valley has differentiated itself from its neighbors (Park City Mountain Resort and Canyons) by delivering a high level of service—including ski valets

DESTINATION

44

and luxurious lodging (like the Stein Eriksen Lodge). "The resort aspires to be the equivalent of a five-star hotel, but on skis," Heidi continued. "Why not have top-level customer service when you come to ski? An amenity like the ski valets (who help unload skis and other equipment) makes it easier on families at a moment in the experience that can be stressful. It sets a nice tone for the day." Deer Valley also limits the number of tickets it sells on a given day to 7,500, even though its lift system can accommodate over fifty thousand skiers per hour. A plethora of grooming equipment assures no shortage of cruisers, though less-tamed terrain is certainly available, especially on Empire and Lady Morgan Mountains. (Deer Valley, incidentally, was the site of several events in the 2002 Olympics, including freestyle moguls, aerials, and alpine slalom.)

Another pleasant service-oriented aspect of Deer Valley—or for that matter, Park City in general: You don't have the hassle of having a car. You can shuttle up to the resorts from Salt Lake City, and there's an excellent bus system in town. "Deer Valley has great ski-in/ski-out lodging," Heidi added, "but if you want to be closer to the action in town, the public transportation system makes it easy."

As the ambassador of skiing for Deer Valley, Heidi is often called upon to ski with guests, and she's ever ready to oblige. When asked to describe an ideal free day on the slopes, she laid out the following itinerary: "Let's say it's a powder day, and I'm going to ski with some friends. I'd plan to meet them at Silver Lake Lodge [located at the base of Bald Mountain] and hop on the Sterling Express chairlift to head to the top. Depending on the snow, I'd jump into either Perseverance or Mayflower Bowl. Then I'd begin making my way west to Empire Canyon; you can make it all the way over without hitting a groomed run. En route, I might hit Ruins of Pompei or Triangle Trees, then Sunset Glade or Ontario Bowl (the latter on Flagstaff Mountain). I'd eventually make my way over to Empire Bowl, and spend the rest of the morning there. One of the great service aspects of Deer Valley is that all of the on-hill dining is first-class. You're not getting a paper plate and a greasy grilled cheese. I have favorite eating spots at each of the lodges, but I think Royal Street Café [midmountain at Silver Lake Village] is my favorite, with the tuna tacos my first choice—they use sushi-grade tuna. In the afternoon, I might do a couple runs on Lady Morgan, maybe Lady Morgan Bowl. Then I'll head back over to Ontario Bowl for an hour or two, as there's usually some fresh spots of snow there. There's an extra hike you can do to get to the very top of Ontario. Most people don't do it. You only gain five or six turns, but the snow is usually not skied out."

One of Heidi's finest Deer Valley memories concerns a run a few years back in Empire Canyon. "I had been at Deer Valley for fourteen years, but I'd never had first tracks at Daly Chutes," she recalled. (The Daly Chutes are ten rock-lined chutes with forty-degree pitches, and a cornice launch to kick everything off.) "There had been so much snow, the area had been closed for avalanche control. I happened to be there the morning it reopened, and was the first person down. When I'd skied it in the past, I'd usually have to stop part of the way down and regroup. This time, the snow was so deep, I couldn't stop. I had the biggest smile on my face as I made my way down. It lasted the rest of the day. I felt like I could be done for the year, it was such a great run."

HEIDI VOELKER was a twelve-year member (1985–97) of the U.S. Ski Team and has competed in the Olympics three times. Heidi also competed three times for the U.S. World Championship team. She has six top-ten World Cup finishes to her credit, including a third-place finish in 1994. Heidi was the 1994 National Champion in giant slalom and finished her racing career with a third-place finish in the giant slalom event at the U.S. Nationals in 1997. She was named Deer Valley's Ambassador of Skiing in 1997. Heidi is the first woman (and living person) to be featured on a Utah license plate. She resides in Park City with her husband, Tim, and their sons, Lucas and Stefan.

If You Go

▶ **Getting There:** Deer Valley is less than an hour from Salt Lake City, which is served by most major carriers.

▶ **Season:** Deer Valley is open early December through mid-April.

▶ **Lift Tickets:** Day tickets begin at $102; multi-day tickets are available. Details are available at www.deervalley.com.

▶ **Level of Difficulty:** Deer Valley is celebrated for having something for everyone. Terrain is classified as 27 percent easier; 41 percent intermediate; 32 percent most difficult.

▶ **Accommodations:** A number of lodging options are available at Deer Valley (800-424-DEER; www.deervalley.com), and just down the road in Park City (800-453-1360; www.visitparkcity.com).

DESTINATION

44

SOLITUDE

RECOMMENDED BY **Dean Roberts**

"If you were to find yourself in an airplane at twelve thousand feet above Solitude, you'd see that it's right in the middle between Alta/Snowbird and Park City," Dean Roberts began. "Though a lot of people may not know Solitude as well as those areas, we experience the same snow; in fact, we get better snow than Park City, as Solitude sits at a higher elevation. All of the resorts benefit from our geographical position relative to the Great Salt Lake. Storms blow in off the Pacific and come across the desert and then the lake. If the water temperature is warmer than the air, we get lake-effect snow like crazy.

"Back when I ran the ski school, I'd say that 20 percent of our business came from Park City. If the snow wasn't so hot over there, guests would go to the front desk at the hotel and ask what to do. The hotel attendants knew the score. They'd say, 'Head over to Solitude. They're higher and the snow is better.' I've worked at Sun Valley, Snow Basin, Alta and Brighton, as well as Solitude. Solitude is my favorite place to ski."

Resting between several more highly publicized neighbors, Solitude has long flown below the radar of all but the locals . . . though word of the mountain sitting twelve miles up Big Cottonwood Canyon has started getting out. Still, the name fits. "Even though it's the closest resort to Salt Lake City [less than thirty miles], Solitude sees light crowds," Dean continued. "There's either no line at the lifts, or a very short one. Since Solitude averages five hundred inches of snow a year, the powder doesn't get tracked out very quickly." Solitude owes both its initial and later prosperity to mining. It was silver mining in the canyon that brought settlers here in the 1870s. As the last mine closed in 1950, seeds for Solitude's future were sown with the arrival of a uranium miner named Robert Barrett. Having made his fortune in Moab, Barrett moved to Salt Lake City and took up skiing. The story goes that, while skiing at Alta one day, he was denied access to the rest-

OPPOSITE:
Professional skier
Rachael Burks
prepares to
drop into
Fantasy Ridge.

DESTINATION

45

rooms. He declared he would open his own resort, and began buying up land in Big Cottonwood Canyon. In the fall of 1957, Solitude opened with two chairlifts.

"I was teaching at Brighton at the time that Solitude was being developed," Dean recalled. "I drove by every day, watching the progress. I heard that they were going to open, so I took the day off so I could ski the first day. My first experience wasn't great. Both of the lifts broke down that opening day. But it got better and better and better. For me, it's as good as it gets." In the mid-1990s, the beginnings of Solitude's European-style village began to take shape; work was completed by 2001.

While it's nice to be able to hang one's hat in Solitude at the end of the day, rather than driving back to Salt Lake or Park City, most would agree that it's the hill, not the amenities, that bring visitors back. That, and the lack of other skiers. Solitude serves up 1,200 acres of terrain; a big plus for families and less-seasoned skiers is that a good part of the mountain (roughly half) is given over to intermediate trails, particularly off the Summit and Eagle Express lifts. If you're new to powder, it's a great place to get your legs. Solitude's deep snow makes it a good venue to dabble in tree skiing. Once your confidence is up, point the boards toward Gary's Glade. "If I'm skiing with intermediates, I like to stay on the village side," Dean added. "Though there's double black terrain up high, most of the lower half is geared toward skiers of average ability. And it tends to be sunny. If I have more advanced skiers, I'd try to get them into Honeycomb Canyon. There are great long runs, terrific glades, and steep pitches." Honeycomb Canyon rests at the northside of Solitude, and requires a bit of a traverse from the Summit Lift; some of Solitude's best vistas are here, including a panorama of Twin Lakes Pass. If you stay on the right side (skier's perspective), you'll find some great tree skiing. If you traverse to the left, you'll encounter open bowls. The farther you go, the fresher the snow!

The attractive though modest-sized village at Solitude is not celebrated for its roaring nightlife. One après-ski activity, however, that will appeal to gourmands is a trip to The Yurt. "Trip" is not an overstatement; to reach The Yurt, guests must cross-country ski or snowshoe for fifteen minutes through a lantern-lit forest. (Guides are provided.) Less than a mile in, you'll come upon the yurt in question, glowing mysteriously against the snow. Chef Mike Richey waits inside. Once you're seated, Chef Richey will prepare a five-course dinner on a free-standing stove as you look on. Recent menu items have included asparagus and lobster crepes, Moroccan spiced duck breast, braised lamb shank, and cabernet poached pear frangipane tart with fresh cream and port reduction.

Note: While snowboarding is permitted at Solitude, most boarders prefer nearby Brighton, which has terrain parks as well as great boarding terrain.

DEAN ROBERTS began skiing at the age of four. He skied at Lead Draw, Idaho, near Pocatello, where a rope tow led to a forty-meter ski jump. While in grade school, he and his pals took their skis to school so they could "fly" off the twelve to fifteen ski jumps they would build between their homes and school. In 1944, when he was in eighth grade, his family moved to Ogden and he headed for Snow Basin. He quickly learned the art of alpine skiing. He was a competitive ski jumper at age seventeen and was a member of both the Weber State and University of Utah alpine ski teams. Dean's ski teaching began in 1957 at Snow Basin. After three years there, he moved to Brighton, where he taught from 1960 to 1963. When the newly established resort of Solitude opened in Big Cottonwood Canyon, Dean joined the ski school there and taught for the Greater Salt Lake Ski School from 1964 to 1969. He became codirector of the Mount Empire Ski School at Solitude in 1969. In 1970, Dean became director of Solitude Ski School, and he and his wife, Kay, oversaw its operations for twenty-five years, until 1994, when he became Solitude's director of skiing. He held this position until 2005. Dean is an honorary lifetime member of the Professional Ski Instructors of America Intermountain Division. The University of Utah's J. Willard Marriott Library's Utah Ski Archives honored Dean with the History-Maker Award in 2003.

If You Go

► **Getting There:** Solitude is in Big Cottonwood Canyon, less then thirty miles from Salt Lake City, which is served by most major carriers.

► **Season:** Solitude is usually open from November 15 through April 15.

► **Lift Tickets:** Day tickets are $72. Multi-day tickets and ski and stay packages are available.

► **Level of Difficulty:** Solitude's sixty-five runs and three bowls are classified as 20 percent beginner; 50 percent intermediate; 30 percent advanced.

► **Accommodations:** A finite amount of slope-side lodging is available in the village of Solitude (800-748-4754; www.skisolitude.com).

DESTINATION

45

JAY PEAK

RECOMMENDED BY JOHN WITHERSPOON

Jay Peak has wound its way around John "Spoon" Witherspoon's life for almost forty years. "I got my start at Jay, though it happened by accident," Spoon recalled. "I was born in Southern California into a decidedly non-skiing family. Through a string of events, my hippie mom ended up in northern Vermont. Though it was 1972, the sixties were still rolling up there; it's the land that time forgot. She ended up taking a job at the old Jay Peak Hotel. Since she was an employee, I got to ski. That got the ball rolling. Eventually, I started teaching at Jay. Not much later, I followed the ski profession out west. I was out there almost twenty years. I was living in Tahoe when I decided to wrap it up on the pro tour and come back home. In many respects, it's pretty much the way I left it."

Jay Peak sits at the northern end of the Green Mountains, some eighty miles northeast of Burlington and a stone's throw from the border with Quebec; some weekends, you may find almost as many Montrealeans as Vermonters on the hill, and both American and Canadian currency are accepted. Named for one of the adjacent towns, which in turn was named for the great New York statesman and first chief justice of the Supreme Court, John Jay, the peak has gained notoriety as home of the East Coast's most substantial snowfall. Jay Peak (with a summit of 3,968 feet) averages a Rockies-like 376 inches of snow annually . . . almost nine feet more than New Hampshire's Mount Washington. (In 2007/8, Jay reported a whopping 419 inches.)

Though many things around Jay hadn't changed over the years that Spoon was away, there was one great transformation: the legitimization and even promotion of tree skiing. "For me, there's a great appeal to skiing the trees," Spoon continued. "It's what Mother Nature intended: Here's a mountain, here's some snow, go ahead. No groomed trails, no gates, no snowmaking. That sense of being in the woods speaks to me in the same way

OPPOSITE:
It was Jay Peak's trees—and the fact that they were opened up for play—that really put it on the map.

DESTINATION

46

big-mountain skiing does—it's skiing au naturel. When I left Vermont to head out west, tree skiing was forbidden at Jay. If you got caught, there would be trouble. Over the past twenty years, they not only began to allow glade skiing, but started creating glades and marketing their presence. Jay has so much space with open hardwood forests and good pitch. It's the kind of environment where you can get way off the trails and get back, or get way out and stay out. When Jay first changed its policies, there was a great outcry in the industry: 'You're sending people into the woods and they're gonna get killed!' Actually, it has gone really well, and now many other mountains have followed suit. Having the trees opened up at Jay gave me something new to explore on my old mountain."

Jay has not only helped popularize glade skiing, the resort has also developed a ski school program to help acclimatize newbies to the trees. "Not surprisingly, a lot of people are daunted by the trees," Spoon said. "I see a lot of people who aren't regulars at Jay. They peer into the glades and then keep going. I've even had very talented skiers—Level II Canadian ski instructors—who couldn't ski the trees. They were great carvers, but carving has nothing to do with skiing in the woods. There, you need a more controlled, skidded turn. I call it 'schmearing.'" (Ski writer Matt Boxler has likened the schmear turn to "a knife scraping warm butter across a piece of toast.") "I also like to teach the hop turn." (The hop turn, incidentally, was pioneered at Jay by Walter Foeger, an Austrian who was instrumental both in fashioning Jay's first trails and in running the early ski education program.) "People who've been working so hard at carving, and may have spent hundreds [or thousands] of dollars in lessons to perfect their form are, understandably, a little resistant. The truth is, you don't have to be an amazing skier to effectively ski the trees. If you're a green-trail skier, we have green woods. If we have an intermediate guy, we can take him into thicker trees that aren't too steep. Of course, if you're more experienced in the glades, we can take you to some gnarly terrain."

One of Spoon's most-recommended Jay Peak tree areas is Beaver Pond Glades. "It's one of the first places they cut when they were creating new glades," Spoon said, "and the cool thing is that it's so wide. The top is pretty steep, but you can cut in lower and take the more pitched parts out of the equation. It's at the edge of the boundary, and you can find a lot of good snow in there." If you do extremely well in Spoon's class—or come into Jay as a skilled glade-iator—you might graduate to Timbuktu, Valhalla, and Beyond Beaver Pond Glade. Jay certainly has its share of challenging inbounds terrain, too. "I like a trail called Staircase," Spoon said. "It's really steep and narrow—a tier of rocks, like giant stairs. If one or two people have gotten there before you, it's not very good. If you're one of the first few people, you're loving it." When you're done playing in Jay's trees (or on the stairs), the retreat of choice is The Belfry. "It's an old one-room schoolhouse, halfway down the access road to town," John added. "It has an old-time lodge feel. There aren't any televisions. It's a conversation bar."

In his recent years back at Jay, Spoon has taken on coaching the kid's free-ski team. It's been a full circle, of sorts. "When I started coaching, the kids weren't superstrong," Spoon said. "They were inching their way along. Then we got two big powder days in a row, fifty inches of snow. There's a little spot that's out-of-bounds where there are some cliffs. I took them back there after that big snow, and the kids were launching themselves off the biggest cliff, stomping the landings clean and rolling out. I was floored. I didn't have a coach when I was growing up. As a young kid, I didn't even realize that there was such a thing as ski racing, though we couldn't have afforded a racing coach anyway. By getting into the industry, I kind of circumnavigated not having a coach when I was a kid. Now I enjoy sharing a little of the knowledge that I gained in my competitive years. Watching the kids that day and seeing how far they'd come was incredibly gratifying."

JOHN "SPOON" WITHERSPOON is a veteran of the Freeskiing World Tour and head freeskiing coach at Jay Peak.

If You Go

▶ **Getting There:** Jay Peak is seventy miles north of Burlington, Vermont, which is served by many carriers.

▶ **Season:** Jay generally is open from Thanksgiving to early May.

▶ **Lift Tickets:** Day tickets run $69; multi-day tickets are available.

▶ **Level of Difficulty:** Jay's seventy-eight trails are rated as 20 percent novice; 40 percent intermediate; 40 percent advanced.

▶ **Accommodations:** Jay Peak Resort (800-451-4449; www.jaypeakresort.com) has a variety of lodging options.

MAD RIVER GLEN

RECOMMENDED BY **Eric Friedman**

Be it on Boston's Storrow Drive or Beverly Hills' Sunset Boulevard, if you sit in enough traffic jams, you'll notice the following bumper sticker:

MAD RIVER GLEN: SKI IT IF YOU CAN

It's a great marketing ploy, but it also speaks to the challenges of a mountain designed for skiing, not as part of a larger vacation juggernaut. (Should you find yourself stalled in traffic in Tel Aviv, Munich, Madrid, Milan, Beijing, Lyon, or Athens, you may find the bumper sticker there, too; it's available in seven languages, in addition to English.)

"Mad River Glen is a ski area, not a resort," Eric Friedman explained. "There's a difference. Ski areas sell lift tickets, resorts sell lots of other stuff. In an age when the ski industry has evolved into a *resort* industry, Mad River Glen is still old-school. It hasn't changed very much since it opened in the late 1940s. The area was started by Roland Palmedo, who was one of the early investors in Stowe. His initial motivation was to bring the mountains of Vermont that he so enjoyed to other people. By the early 1940s, he had become disenchanted with how commercial Stowe had become. He wanted to create a place where skiing was the focus. Palmedo was a pilot, and he flew over the Green Mountains looking for the perfect spot to establish a new ski area. He found it above the village of Waitsfield. When you're at the top of Mad River Glen and look north, you can't see Stowe, as another mountain—Camel's Hump—blocks the view. The story goes that one reason Palmedo chose this site was so you couldn't see Mount Mansfield!"

Not a great deal has changed since the mountain opened for business in 1948. "In the early days—through the 1950s and '60s—Mad River Glen went toe-to-toe with the other big ski areas in New England," Eric continued. "But as the industry changed, we stayed the same. It's very noncommercial. You won't see any banners for an 'official vehicle' or

OPPOSITE:
A skier goes
it alone on
Mad River Glen's
fabled Single
Chair.

DESTINATION

47

'official beer.' It doesn't happen, and people appreciate that. And you won't see snowboarders any time soon. The area is owned by a co-op, and the 2,200 owners have never shown any interest in opening up the mountain to boarders. In some ways, Mad River is a living museum of the ski industry." (In fact, Mad River Glen is now the only ski area in the nation on the National Registry of Historic Places—not the lodge, but the ski area itself.)

One shouldn't mistake a commitment to preservation and history as a sign of present-day calcification. As its bumper sticker implies, Mad River has more than its share of challenging terrain. "I like to think of Mad River as the flyweight boxer of downhill skiing," Eric said. "At its peak, the mountain is just 3,600 feet. But our two thousand vertical feet are, pound for pound, one of the world's toughest ski experiences. Mad River has forty-five marked trails. But when the snow is good, you ski the glades next to the trails. I love to take people from out West or Europe out on the mountain. I'll often hear even the cocky ones say, 'I can't believe the skiing on this little mountain.' (In total, the area offers 115 acres of trail skiing, plus 800 acres of boundary-to-boundary tree skiing.)

"One thing that sets the terrain at Mad River Glen apart is that you get two thousand feet vertical with one chairlift. They don't build many two-thousand-foot vertical lifts, and this one gets you to the top in nine or ten minutes—it's the fastest fixed-grip lift in North America. Another thing that's special is that the mountain is all sustained vertical, with no run-outs. You can jump off a cliff on a double black diamond run and land right in the lift line! If we have a decent powder day, I'll take the Single Chair up and ski Fall Line and Paradise—or ski my favorite run on the hill, a spot in between the two that we call Falldise—and head right back down to the Single Chair."

Though there's some well-deserved bravado associated with Mad River Glen, there are facets of the ski area that have appeal to skiers of more modest ability. "It's true that we don't sell a lot of beginner packages," Eric continued, "but some people who spend time here feel it's the ultimate family ski area. There's not as many people as on some hills in the area, and that can help make it a more positive experience for less skilled skiers. I think parents also appreciate the noncommercial vibe. We have a reputation for runs that can make your butt pucker, we have lots of good intermediate terrain as well."

Ski aficionados who may know little about the runs at Mad River may know a bit more about the area's most-fabled icon: its single chairlift. It certainly holds fond memories for Eric. "Back in 2001, we realized that our single chair, which had been in operation since 1948, needed to be rebuilt or replaced," he recalled. "The co-op shareholders considered the various options: a brand-new single, a brand-new double, a gondola. After several years of deliberation, they decided that we should do a historic restoration of the lift, even though it was considerably more expensive than putting in a brand-new single or double lift. We hired a consultant to spearhead the fund-raising. He thought we'd be able to raise $700,000 or $800,000 of the projected $1.8 million cost. We raised the whole $1.8 million, plus enough to establish a healthy maintenance fund.

"My most memorable Mad River moment came when rides on the old single chair were being auctioned off to raise funds. I outbid a guy for the lift's last four rides. Two were for my sons, one was for me, and the last one was for Ken Quackenbush, who was general manager of the area for forty-five years. Ken is the only guy who has a trail named after him on the mountain. He was ninety at the time. In my office, I have a picture of Ken at the top of the mountain. He represents what's so special about Mad River Glen: family, camaraderie, and the love we share for the mountain."

(Regrettably, Ken Quackenbush passed away in March 2012, at the age of ninety-six.)

ERIC FRIEDMAN has been the marketing director for Mad River Glen since the co-op's inception in 1995. He comes from a long line of great Jewish skiers from New Jersey and currently lives just a bit downhill from the mountain in a 210-year-old farmhouse with his two sons, who represent Mad River Glen's next generation of rippers.

If You Go

▶ **Getting There:** Mad River Glen is in Waitsfield, Vermont, roughly 45 minutes south of Burlington, which is served by many carriers.

▶ **Season:** There's generally enough snow to ski from mid-December to early April. See up-to-date ski reports at www.madriverglen.com.

▶ **Lift Tickets:** Full-day tickets range from $49 (mid-week) to $72 (holidays).

▶ **Level of Difficulty:** Nearly half the slopes are black diamond; however, there's plenty of novice and intermediate terrain, too.

▶ **Accommodations:** Mad River offers a number of ski and stay packages with local inns; visit www.madriverglen.com/lodging for details.

DESTINATION

47

STOWE

RECOMMENDED BY **Jeff Wise**

Jeff Wise likes to say that he found Stowe by falling out of the sky.

"Twenty years ago, I was doing advertising sales for an alternative rock station in New York City," Jeff began. "However, I always loved Vermont. I would always go in on a ski house in southern Vermont with friends, usually at Mount Snow. I'd drive up religiously on Friday nights and ski the weekend. In the fall of 1993, I decided that I wanted to change jobs and try living in Vermont. I made plans to attend a job fair at Mount Snow, and a friend who had a small plane offered to fly me up. The day we flew, we couldn't land the plane in the Dover, as there were strong crosswinds. It was a clear day, and we could see Route 100 below and started following it north, taking in the foliage. Eventually, we saw a very small airport, and got permission to land. We found out we were in Morrisville. I had never been north of Killington [a ski area near Rutland, Vermont]. In the little town, I asked if there was a good place to have lunch, and someone said, 'Stowe's just down the road.' The second I laid eyes on it, I said, 'Wow!' I was getting ready to move to a ski town in Vermont, and here was a ski town that's a real town, not a resort with an access road. I walked around town and went up to the resort to inquire about getting a job as a snowboard instructor. By the time I got back to New York, there was no question I'd be heading north."

The town of Stowe sits just northeast of Burlington, the state's most populous city; the ski area (technically known as Stowe Mountain Resort) takes up the eastern flank of Mount Mansfield, Vermont's highest summit at 4,395 feet. (The lift-served area tops out at 3,719 feet.) Like many ski areas in the Alps, Stowe had its start as an actual town (first settled in 1794) and later as a summer escape. "The first hotels opened in the 1850s and a toll road was built up to Mount Mansfield shortly thereafter," Jeff continued. "Stowe had

OPPOSITE:

For many, Stowe defines New England skiing.

been welcoming visitors for almost a hundred years before the ski resort was established, and I think your first and last impression is that Stowe is authentic, not contrived."

Stowe is not the oldest ski resort in the United States, though it certainly helped set the tone for the sport's early development. The first official trails on Mount Mansfield were cut by the Civilian Conservation Corps (CCC) in 1933. The following year, the first ski patrol was established there (it provided a model for the National Ski Patrol), and Stowe hosted the U.S. Eastern Amateur Association Downhill and the Men's and Women's National Downhill and Slalom championships in 1937 and 1938, respectively. Both were held on a trail called Nose Dive, which was designed by an unemployed highway engineer named Charlie Lord, with the help of his friend Abner Coleman. There was a time when Nose Dive was considered the most fearsome trail in the country.

"Mount Mansfield is very well-suited to snowboarding and skiing, as there's two thousand vertical feet of consistent pitch," Jeff said. "Most of the trails were cut by hand, following the natural fall line of the mountain. On some hills, you can tell that a bulldozer went straight down the hill and there's not much character to the skiing/riding experience. At Stowe, they twist and turn naturally. Though it's not a large mountain, there are steeps that match those at other, bigger areas. If there's a section of the mountain that defines the Stowe experience, it's the Front Four: Liftline, National, Starr, and Goat. All are rated double black diamond, and that's a legitimate double black. Each has a consistent pitch ranging from twenty-six to thirty-eight degrees, though each poses a different kind of challenge. Liftline might be the easiest of the four, as it's fairly wide, and the left side gets some grooming; though as the name implies, you're right under the Forerunner Quad, and have lots of spectators. National got its name from the fact that several ski-racing championships were held on the trail. If there's enough snow, it can be one of the premiere mogul runs in the East. Starr is named for C. V. Starr, who founded AIG, the insurance giant. The view from the top of the trail is harrowing; it's so steep, you seem to stare off into nothingness. Goat is the steepest and narrowest of the four, and has huge moguls." Visitors who hope to conquer the Front Four are encouraged to leave Goat for last.

Beyond the challenge of the Front Four, one of the appeals of Stowe is the variety of accommodations and things to do in town once you're off the slopes. "There's everything from roadside motels to unique resort properties like the Trapp Family Lodge. If you recall the movie *The Sound of Music*, the family flees Austria at the conclusion. They actually relocated to Stowe and eventually opened a lodge and cross-country ski center, and they are still here. AIG [which owns Stowe Mountain Resort] recently constructed the Stowe Mountain Lodge, which has been getting incredible accolades, and brings a new level of luxury to the mix. The town has more than twenty-five restaurants and watering holes, so you have lots of options."

One of Stowe's most famous trails is one you won't find on any trail maps—the Bruce Trail. This is the first trail at Stowe cut specifically for skiing, created in 1933 by the CCC. "Skiing the Bruce Trail is one of the most special things you can do at Stowe," Jeff shared, "though technically, it takes you outside the resort boundary." (Vermont state law requires that you pay for your own rescue if you are injured skiing outside the resort's boundary.) "The Bruce Trail is four miles long. It takes you from the top of the Forerunner Quad, all the way to the Cross-Country Ski Center. In fact, you can practically ski all the way to Matterhorn Bar, which is the quintessential ski-town bar, with a wood-fired pizza oven, sushi bar, pool tables, and live music.

"My hypothetical best day on the mountain would end with me making fresh tracks on the Bruce down to the Matterhorn, and heading in for a refreshment. Legally, we don't encourage people to do this. But it's there."

JEFF WISE was director of Stowe Mountain Resort's Snowboard School for five years before becoming the resort's marketing and communications director.

If You Go

▶ **Getting There:** Stowe is less than an hour from Burlington, which is served by many carriers.
▶ **Season:** Stowe's season usually runs from late November to mid-April.
▶ **Lift Tickets:** Advance day tickets are $79; multi-day tickets are available. Learn more at www.stowe.com.
▶ **Level of Difficulty:** Stowe's 116 trails are rated as 16 percent beginner; 59 percent intermediate; 25 percent expert.
▶ **Accommodations:** Stowe Area Association (877-GOSTOWE; www.gostowe.com) and Stowe Mountain Resort (800-253-4754; www.stowe.com) offer a variety of lodging options.

MOUNT BAKER

RECOMMENDED BY **Tom Monterosso**

"There is a place in the ski and snowboard world for full-blown resorts," Tom Monterosso ventured. "The full mountain experience—condos, food courts, ice-skating rinks, and the rest—is just right for some, especially the more casual rider. But if you have $500 to spend, and you want to stretch it as far as you can and ride your heart out, Mount Baker is for you. For as big as the terrain at Baker is, the mountain—and the surrounding area—hasn't crazily expanded. There aren't any five-star hotels with hot tubs the size of small towns. You don't find the kind of amenities that pull your attention away from the hill, and for me, that's what it's about."

Mount Baker rises roughly thirty miles east (as the crow flies) from Bellingham, Washington, near the Canadian border. At 10,781 feet, the volcano (second most active in the Cascades after St. Helens to the south) is in view on a clear day from as far west as Vancouver Island and as far south as Tacoma. Baker is renowned as one of the snowiest places in the world; it averages 701 inches a year; in the winter of 1998/99, the mountain accumulated a remarkable 1,140 inches (nearly the height of a ten-story office building, if you're counting!). The portion of the mountain where the resort operates is not terribly high, registering 4,300 feet at the top of the Heather Meadows area and 3,500 feet at the White Salmon area, with a vertical drop of 1,500 feet. Yet, these statistics can be misleading. Professional snowboarder Lucas Debare, who calls Baker his home hill, described it as like a skate park, with features everywhere to appeal to different styles of snowboarding. Thanks to the coastal snow, there's relatively low avalanche danger. The inbounds terrain is unrivaled, with runs as gnarly as you could desire. The backcountry seems to go on forever. (Baker offers one thousand acres of terrain.)

OPPOSITE:
Mount Baker offers incredible backcountry terrain. Here, some off-piste enthusiasts stand in the shadow of Mt. Shuksan.

"If I were to be at Baker on a bluebird day with fresh snow, I'd first head to Chair Five, one of the most famous lifts in snowboarding," Tom continued. "There's so much amazing inbounds terrain here. [For example, the chute-riddled Gabl's.] I'd lap that for a while, make some turns, and then grab my avalanche gear and head over to the out-of-bounds area near Hemispheres. It's world-class, some of the best out-of-bounds terrain anywhere. You could ride for a year and not come close to covering it all."

The event that helped put Mount Baker on the snowboarding map is the Mount Baker Banked Slalom (known in some circles as the Legendary Banked Slalom). First held in 1985, the five-hundred-foot-long course featured fifteen gates; the winner received (and still receives) a trophy fashioned from duct tape. (The event was held at Mount Baker, incidentally, because few other mountains were allowing snowboarders at the time.) "Growing up on the East Coast, I never had the money to come out to Washington and participate, though I was certainly aware of the event," Tom continued. "It was in the top three on my bucket list. During my first year working at *Snowboarder* magazine, I told my editor how I'd always wanted to go up to the Banked Slalom, to run the race, eat the smoked salmon, attend the parties. I got the green light and I was off to Mount Baker.

"There are several things that make the event special. The Banked Slalom is the only snowboarding event where members from all the different boarding communities intermingle—rail kids, pipe kids, mountain freestylers. You'll be standing at the top and to your left you'll see Wolfgang Nyvelt, to your right, Danny Davis. Up-and-comers can hang with old-guard riders like Tom Burt. It's also the only contest in snowboarding where you never have to leave the ground, where you don't have to do any tricks. Whoever turns the best and goes the fastest wins. The Banked Slalom captures the whole vibe of Mount Baker. People don't need the latest gear or ride the latest trend. They wear clothes that are functional. They are there to ride.

"Incidentally, on that first trip, I finished dead last in the qualifying event. That may have been because it had snowed approximately six feet in two days, and I'd been lapping the best snow I'd ever experienced the whole day leading up to my run on the course!"

If there's an unofficial post-riding gathering spot for Mount Baker snowboarders, many would say that it's Milanos, an Italian restaurant (with a fine snowboarding pedigree) in the little town of Glacier. "I'll never forget my first visit to Milanos," Tom said. "During the day, I'd ridden the deepest powder I'd ever experienced. It was my first Baker Banked Slalom, and everyone I knew in the snowboarding world was there on the mountain. A group of us went down to Glacier, the nearest town, for dinner. There's just one strip of asphalt, one bar, one snowboard shop, and one restaurant. Milanos is partly owned by the Debare family, a clan that's nothing short of Mount Baker royalty. The Debare children, Lucas and Maria, are big-name pros. All of my friends were there drinking beer at the bar. Eventually we had an amazing Italian dinner, and got to meet Lucas's mom, the queen of Mount Baker."

A perfect ending to a perfect day.

Tom Monterosso is senior editor of *Snowboarder* magazine.

If You Go

▶ **Getting There:** Mount Baker is roughly an hour east of Bellingham, Washington, which is served by Alaska Airlines (800-252-7522; www.alaskaair.com), Allegiant Air (702-505-8888; www.allegiantair.com), and Frontier Airlines (800-432-1359; www .flyfrontier.com).

▶ **Season:** The season generally runs from mid-November to late April. See up-to-date ski reports at www.mtbaker.us.

▶ **Lift Tickets:** Full-day tickets are $47 to $52; multi-day tickets are available.

▶ **Level of Difficulty:** Nearly a third of Mount Baker's terrain is considered advanced or expert. The Baker Banked Slalom is generally held in mid-February.

▶ **Accommodations:** A number of lodging options are listed on the Mount Baker Ski Area website (www.mtbaker.us).

JACKSON HOLE

RECOMMENDED BY **Matt Hansen**

"There are resorts that have lots of snow," Matt Hansen ventured, "and areas that have backcountry gates and gnarly terrain with significant vertical. But at Jackson, you have it all. There's nowhere else where you can get the vertical, the backcountry terrain, and the snow that Jackson Hole has to offer . . . and that's what makes it so special for die-hard, expert skiers. I had fallen in love with it as a kid, before I even skied there. I'd traveled up there in the summer with my family, and I had this vision of Jackson skiing from movies and photos, a place of steep mountains and deep snow. I wasn't disappointed."

Jackson Hole Mountain Resort rests in the Tetons—perhaps America's most iconic mountain range—just south of Grand Teton National Park. (For the record, the resort is in Teton Village, not Jackson; and Jackson Hole refers not to the town, but to the fifty-mile valley that lies to the east of the mountains.) Jackson Hole's terrain is spread over two mountains: Apres Vous has the lion's share of the area's easier terrain; Rendezvous has everything else, and is the mountain that defines Jackson for most comers. There are places that get more snow than Jackson, but with an average of almost forty feet, good coverage is not an issue. The area's 4,100-plus feet of continuous vertical is shared between 2,500 acres of inbounds terrain and another 3,000 acres that can be accessed through the backcountry gates. Its bowls, couloirs, and cliffs are the stuff of legend. "With the tram, you can climb the whole 4,100 feet in one fell swoop," Matt continued. "It only takes twelve minutes. Not only do you have a vast network of inbounds terrain that's steep and technical, but you can get to the backcountry."

Jackson Hole is the kind of area that inspires a fanatical commitment. Matt is certainly a believer. "My first time skiing Jackson Hole was on New Year's Day in 1996. My friends and I were all hungover, and it was raining out. Conditions were terrible. Future

OPPOSITE:
Local pro A.J.
Cargill drops into
the infamous
couloir, "Once
Is Enough."

DESTINATION

50

visits showed the mountain in all its glory, and I moved to Jackson in 1998, right after college. I was pretty poor that first winter, and slept on a Therm-a-Rest in my sleeping bag in a room I shared with a hippie friend. Still, I fell in love with it. Being surrounded by those beautiful mountains is part of the appeal, but it's also the culture. People are there to be outside, whether it's skiing, fishing, or mountaineering."

Jackson Hole's most famous trail—though, in Matt's opinion, not its most difficult—is Corbet's Couloir. This vertiginously steep chute was named for Barry Corbet, founder of Jackson Hole Mountain Guides; the story goes that when he and Paul McCollister (the area's initial developer) made their way up Rendezvous Mountain for McCollister's first descent, Corbet spied the couloir and declared that "Someday someone will ski that—it will be a run." (A ski patrolman named Lonnie Ball is believed to be the first person to ski Corbet's; Barry did eventually run his namesake couloir.) Many who gaze over the precipice simply lose their nerve, as the first move you face is a two-story drop onto a fifty-five-degree slope. If you don't carve a right turn quickly enough, you come face-to-face with a rock wall. If you survive these initial turns, the remainder of the run, with a "modest" forty-degree pitch, will seem easy. "Corbet's is the test piece of Jackson," Matt explained. "It's very exposed, as you're right under the tram. You're on a stage, and it's nerve-racking, as you don't want to screw up. In a lot of ways, that's what makes it so difficult."

Though inbounds trails like Corbet's Couloir will provide more challenge than most can bite off, aficionados believe that it's Jackson's backcountry that really makes it shine. Oddly enough, the three thousand backcountry acres were only made available during the 1999/2000 season—though that's not to say that they didn't see tracks in previous years. "Before the boundaries opened, you had the Jackson Hole Air Force, a group of ski bums that would poach the out-of-bounds areas," Matt said. "These guys were engaged in a constant cat-and-mouse game with the ski patrol, cops, and other authority figures." The Air Force's lead instigators—Bennie Wilson, Howie Henderson, and Doug Coombs—became infamous for eavesdropping on ski patrol radio channels, constructing small on-mountain huts (to hide from patrollers), and otherwise conspiring to lead fellow scofflaws to the powder on north-facing Granite Canyon and other beyond-the-gates areas. Members of the Air Force could once be identified by a tiny pin, bearing a skull, crossed ski poles, and the legend "Swift. Silent. Deep. 1st Tracks OB. JHAF."

"For me, Jackson Hole is all about the backcountry, " Matt continued. "Granite Canyon is one of the most beautiful places I've ever skied. You need to take avalanche gear, and you need to know how to use it. Once you're beyond the gate, there are dozens of chutes you can take. You need to know where you're going, as it's serious stuff; some of the chutes end in death cliffs. But in a clean run, you're in among these big cliffs and spires that are covered with different-colored lichens. You're on the north face of an enormous canyon, and you feel very small, like an ant. From here, it's a two-thousand-vertical-foot drop. The snow is usually great in here—knee-deep powder. You don't want to stop along the way, as you're vulnerable to what might fall from above, so you keep going. There's a little creek at the bottom. To get back to the resort, you have to traverse forty-five minutes. It's pretty burly, almost all side-stepping.

"When I'm hiking about in the Tetons, away from the tram—that's why I became a skier. I'm thankful my parents taught me how to ski when I was young. Having built up my knowledge and skills, I've been able to go out and do something that's filled with risk and danger—but that gives me a sense of being alive."

MATT HANSEN is a writer and editor whose primary focus is on skiing deep snow, and the culture that surrounds it. Assignments have taken him across the globe and back again, but his refuge of deepness will always be in the Tetons. He is currently an editor at large for *Powder* magazine and a consultant for Atomic Skis.

If You Go

▶ **Getting There:** Jackson is served by several airlines, including American (800-433-7300; www.aa.com) and United Airlines (800-864-8331; www.united.com).

▶ **Season:** Jackson Hole is generally open from late November through early April.

▶ **Lift Tickets:** Full-day tickets range from $74 to $99. Visit www.jacksonhole.com for details.

▶ **Level of Difficulty:** Jackson is known as a mountain for advanced skiers and the 116 named trails reinforce this perception: 10 percent beginner; 40 percent intermediate; 50 percent expert.

▶ **Accommodations:** A broad variety of lodging options around Jackson Hole are listed at www.jacksonhole.com.

DESTINATION

50

Published in 2013 by ABRAMS

Text copyright © 2013 Chris Santella

Photograph credits: Page 16: Mark Fisher/Fisher Creative; Page 20: Adam Clark; Page 24: Henry Georgi;
Page 28: Photo courtesy Keoki Flagg/GalleryKeoki.com; Page 34: Adam Clark; Page 42: ©Copyright TVB
St. Anton am Arlberg/photographer Josef Mallaun; Page 48: Topher Donahue/CMH Heli-Skiing; Page 52:
©Scott Markewitz; Page 56: Adam Clark; Page 60: Adam Clark; Page 64: ©Scott Markewitz; Page 70: Adam
Clark; Page 74: Adam Clark; Page 78: ©Scott Markewitz; Page 82: ©Scott Markewitz; Page 86: Photo: Tom Stillo;
Page 90: Adam Clark; Page 94: Larry Pierce; Page 100: ©Christian Aslund/Lonely Planet Images/Getty Images;
Page 104: Jack Affleck ©Vail Resorts; Page 108: ©Scott Markewitz; Page 112: ©Scott Markewitz; Page 116:
Tory Taglio; Page 124: ©Scott Markewitz; Page 128: ©Scott Markewitz; Page 136: ©Scott Markewitz; Page 140:
Greg Keeler/Cannon Mountain; Page 144: www.tucman.com; Page 148: J. Kevin Foltz/
Taos Ski Valley; Page 152: Adam Clark; Page 156: Harris Mountain Heli Ski, Photo: Larry Prosor; Page 160:
Christian Aslund/Photographer's Choice/Getty Images; Page 164: Brian Becker; Page 168: Michael G. Halle;
Page 172: The credit is: Le Massif de Charlevoix / Alain Blanchette; Page 176: ©Walter Bibikow/The Image Bank/
Getty Images; Page 180: "Skiers on the Kamchatka Peninsula" Photo credit: Elemental Adventure; Page 184:
Adam Clark; Page 188: ©Leo Julen; Page 194: ©Scott Markewitz; Page 200: Adam Clark; Page 204: Bryan Smith/
Jay Peak Resort; Page 208: Jeb Wallace-Brodeur; Page 212: Stowe Mountain Resort; Page 216: Adam Clark;
Page 220: Mark Fisher/Fisher Creative

Library of Congress Control Number: 2013935969

ISBN: 978-1-61769-054-9

Editor: Samantha Weiner
Designer: Anna Christian
Production Manager: Tina Cameron
Fifty Places series design by Paul G. Wagner

This book was composed in Interstate, Scala, and Village.

Printed and bound in China
10 9 8
ABRAMS books are available at special discounts when purchased in quantity for premiums
and promotions as well as fundraising or educational use. Special editions can also be created to specification.
For details, contact specialsales@abramsbooks.com or the address below.

ABRAMS The Art of Books
195 Broadway, New York, NY 10007
abramsbooks.com